EXISTENTIAL RUMINATIONS

𝔉𝔬𝔯𝔢𝔴𝔬𝔯𝔡

REVIEWS   THE INDIE WE LOVE.

Existential Ruminations

Existential Ruminations is a thought-provoking, philosophical poetry collection that muses through looming issues in a personalized manner.

Inspired by teleportation and an experience of divine intervention, the poems and philosophical ruminations collected in Gentry Thomason's book *Existential Ruminations* are intriguing as they investigate the meaning of life.

Split into thematic sections, these prose poems, or "poemographs," are brief (none more than fourteen lines), committed to their individual subjects, and spiritual. They are preceded by a lengthy introduction explaining their genesis and defending the rationale behind their structures. Though the subsequent entries are lineated and flowed like poetry, they evade lyricism and symbolism in favour of direct, unadorned streams of thought; their language is forthright and precise.

Some entries are personal (one declares "When I was younger, ages 20 to 50, / my pursuit of individuality / was strong within me"); some address the audience in a direct manner, or make grand proclamations like "We are all parochial in myriad ways!" Photographs are present to complement the book's personal references. Together, the poems form a book that is cosmic in scope, covering truth, identity, religion, and other weighty topics; It is best consumed in small doses.

"Being (in the World)" ruminates how the set of circumstances that create the trajectory of a person's life are all a matter of chance:

> *Consider coming into existence*
> *in the world:*
> *If you are born into a troubled place*
> *life could be hazardous and very fragile*
> *with many possible deaths*
> *dotting the landscape*
> *--even in a most peaceful place*
> *death could snatch your unawares*
> *by dint of car or cancer*
> *or multiple opportunities for violence...*

Though its entries are often religious in bent, they are also prone to addressing philosophical objections to the idea of the existence and benevolence of God. References are made to the Holocaust and other forms of evil that the poems acknowledge make it difficult to accept traditional religious understandings of being. The reality of death is also confronted, with entries circling back to the inevitability of decline and decay. This consciousness of the dark sides of existence and the persistence of doubt are intriguing.

...Existential Rumination is an often thought-provoking, philosophical poetry collection that muses through looming issues in a personalized manner.

MATT BENZING CRITICS (January 23, 2023)

EXISTENTIAL RUMINATIONS

Gentry Thomason

ARPress
45 Dan Road Suite 15
Canton MA 02021

| Hotline: | 1(888) 821-0229 |
| Fax: | 1(508) 545-7580 |

Ordering Information:

Quantity sales. Special discounts are available on quantity purchases by corporations, associations, and others. For details, contact the publisher at the address above.

Printed in the United States of America.

| ISBN-13: | Softcover: 979-8-89389-702-9 |
| | eBook: 979-8-89389-703-6 |

Library of Congress Control Number: 2024922580

Dedication

To all I have loved, admired,
and held in high esteem ––
God bless you
(living and deceased)

Insignificant mortals, who are as leaves,
and feed on what the ground gives,
but then fade away and are dead.
> Homer, The Iliad

Hope springs eternal in the human breast;
Man never is, but always to be blest.
> Alexander Pope,
> An Essay on Man

The first hope in our inventory—the hope
that includes and at the same time transcends
all others—must be the hope that love is going
to have the last word.
> Arnold J. Toynbee,
> "Conditions of Survival,"
> Saturday Review'

Turn Your Radio On*
> Ray Stevens

Contents

Section One
Existence and Eternity

Section Two
Truth and Reality

Section Three

God, Religion, and the Supernatural

Section Four
Self and Others

Section Five

Character, Love, and Vision

Preface

Existential
(ruminations)

What is an individual existence?
A multitude of variant experiences
thoughts and feelings and aspirations
that constitute the complex of living
with family, friends and sometime associates
and inner experiences of random uniqueness
that spell the quantity and quality
of myriad moments and paths developing
that individual life, its total trajectory
from birth to death and all intermediates
that do enumerate some tolerable significance
in the encompassing scheme of things
with demarcations of the spirit
in mind and thoughts
and cavernous reflections.

Immense
(insignificance)

In my mind my life is a very big deal
of which I am conscious nearly 24/7
but the astronomers tell me that the earth
on which I live 24/7 is an insignificant dot
a little blue pin prick in an infinite sea
of a universe that may be an insignificant dot
in a multi-universe that has no ending
which makes me aware that my busy little mind
must not be a very big deal at all
is even an infinitesimally small pale sea
of absolutely no consequence or significance
in an infinitesimally small insignificant universe
that may be of absolutely no importance
in a multi-universe that has
no breadth or boundary
??????????????
?

Existential
(sound sense)

Each of us acts and operates
with the belief our behaviors are meaningful
for if we didn't life would be negated
and turned into a meaningless travesty
where responsibilities would not be honored
and human interactions would be senseless:
The glue that holds human life together
is the credibility of human relatedness
and the serious devotion of one to another
whence life does coalesce in healthy community:
Trustworthy and reliable sociability
is the result of character constitution
that endears each to all and vice-versa
which makes for communal coherence:
Is this reasoning not existential sound sense?

Experiential
(is Existential)

The facticity of human experience
resolves itself in moments of expression
in language that identifies
and defines its character and qualities of reality
to reality of having been lived
in the world of our being and becoming:
Such experiencing is patently existential
in that it is part and parcel of existence.
Experience is therefore existential
and grounded in everyday living reality.
Existential in its generic sense
is thus common to all living persons:
All persons are existential beings
who live in our world of common reality:
Experiential is existential!

Now
(and forever)

I am now in my early eighties
––still a kid, still young at heart––
but have lived just long enough
to have settled on
some thoughts and feelings:
What you shall find here
are my musing on life and eternity
the latter now more pressing upon me
as I anticipate my looming exit
from this life––my existence in it:
None of us gets to live forever
in this world we find ourselves
––we must struggle with our identities
their highs and lows and in-betweens
for better or worse––now and forever.

Existence
(precedes Essence)

In his essay "Existentialism"
Philosopher Jean-Paul Sartre
says that "existence precedes essence".
Well, what is existence?
Existence is human existence
living human existence in the world.
Existence begins in innocent infancy
progresses through the years of childhood
to adolescence and then to young adulthood
operating always in the world.
Such process of growth involves aspirations
the reaching for things to satisfy one's spirit.
Even into maturity and ultimate old age
one seeks for essence
--one's **spiritual** essence.

Introduction

I published *Rogues' Gallery* in the first decade of our current century, the year 2007 to be precise. Subsequent to that book's being published I continued to write what I fashioned, in that book, the term for my particular kind of inditing——"poemographs"——which are expressions of *thoughts* that have weighed in upon me, my interior being, most of my life but especially in these later years of my existence on this planet.

The style and fashion of my poemographs are attempts to articulate my *thoughts* in some *rhythmical* manner that approximate recognizable ordinary speech. Each line of each poemograph seeks to give voice to the flow of thought of the ideas contained in each construct. I do not typically employ poetic artifice in these poemographs.

It is my aim and intention to communicate to my readers clearly accessible thoughts and feelings——not cleverly ornate expressions loaded with literary ingenuity. No one should confuse my poemographs with the style and artistry of an Emily Dickinson or a Stephen Crane. I am not myself confused in any of this. I do not consider my style of writing to be marked by high literary artifice or distinction. Far from it: The *ideas* are the *thing*.

My poemographs began to evolve into a fourteen line framework which I absorbed from the English sonnet form: Most ideas, I have found, can be briefly expressed and contained in that number of lines although occasionally the expression runs longer but rarely much shorter (as in many of my *Rogues' Gallery* poemographs). The effort has been to be succinct (concise) and not long-winded.

The range and scope of my thinking is comprehensible in the five section titles: Existence and Eternity; Truth and Reality; God, Religion and the Supernatural; Self and Others; Character, Love and Vision. Those were the broad categories I discovered to be where my head and heart lay (over the several years of inditing) when I sought to compile my numerous poemographs into book form. Those categories advanced upon the sections of *Rogues' Gallery*: symbolic (elements); double (binders); figurative (expressions); battle (ments); method (ologies). Perhaps my more recent thinking has been pressed by my advancing age and my approaching transition to another realm of existence.

What I have articulated in this volume is something like a summation of what life has been about for me and what most of us sense and grasp as we advance in age and maturity. All of us will eventually depart from this world and leave it behind. And many of us, I suspect, will be hoping for some kind of agreeable reality in some kind of agreeable future. I think that kind of hope and expectation is endemic to being human. Some, in their advanced thinking and surmising, may disagree with that hope and expectation, but I would enjoin even those to give some labor to exploring what I have to say. I categorize and place my thoughts in the arena of the common human enterprise.

We come into this world hopefully invited and hopefully exit as gracefully as possible without too much crying and gasping. We inevitably rest in the hands of others––and should, I think, refrain from excluding the hands of Providence in our exits. Should we then, in our exits, reach another dimension of life and reality, we should hope it would be a joyous and pleasant one. Who would disagree with that anticipation?

Scholars have labored over such prospects and realities for centuries––frankly, and most probably, since beings of all humanoid stripes have roamed this planet as conscious and sentient. There exists a formidable and growing literature on such reflection, always, however, grounded in a sober speculation in the scholar or his or her reflective recipients. Is there any way to get around such thinking? What is life and reality all about? We know in every individual human being there is a starting and a stopping point: Such reality can only be avoided by *refusing* to give one's self to thought. Isn't all thinking a genesis for growth? Can we really *refuse* to submit ourselves to this endeavor in our maturity? Life itself, I believe, leads us in this direction. Thus the soldier in each of us should march?

Much of the content in this volume had its origin in a moment of experience in San Diego, California in August of 1979. My initial expression of that moment was as follows:

8/'79: TURNIN'

Drivin' south on Genesee
'Bout thirty mile an hour
Had wound around from Regents
Was feelin' kinda down
Been comin' from confession
Way up on Govenor Drive
Our Mother of Confidence
Catholic Church
Felt like I was 'gonna die
The priest had passed forgiveness
Myself I hadn't though
Was strugglin' for survival
Against an ugly foe—
And then I hit a darkened stretch
Drove into valley dip
Came out 'bout three secs later
Four mile other way—no fits
I calmly assessed the condition
Of this 'mazin turn about
Knew it couldn't happen in Nature
'Cause her laws don't work like that
So I made my turn at the stop light

And headed back home again
Feelin' mighty strange and curious
How this thing could have been
Then later came Ol' demon
'Bout like to give me fits
But he drove me back to Jesus
Now ain't that a funny fix?

That poem was written as a companion piece to an earlier experience I had on the Kansas Turnpike in late 1964:

10/'64: TRAVELIN'

Rollin' down the freeway
'Bout seventy mile an hour
Barrelin' on a straight stretch
Feelin' kinda proud
Sense a funny wobblin'
Think the right front tire
Ease up on the gas a bit
Steer the wheel to south
Lose control completely
Hit the medial hard
Bounce and flip and turn about
Three time 'round and 'round
Wind up in the culvert
Left side smashed way in
Facin' opposite direction
Wonderin' wildly——how?
Climb up out of 'mobile
Shake a hand or two
Notice nothin' 'nusual
'Til patrolman tells it true:
Ol' A-frame sheared too smooth:
Takes me thirty minutes
To get the 'drenlin blues
Start to shake and feelin' pale
Finally realize, too,

Ol' highway not the place
this day
To pay my deathly dues.

I had just completed Army Officer Candidate School and Airborne Training (jump school/parachuting) and had driven from Fort Benning, Georgia to Liberty, Missouri, my original hometown, and was heading west-southwest to San Diego, California where my parents were living. I had purchased a 1962 Corvair in Columbus, Georgia (the automobile that Ralph Nader had written a book about) and was not "up on" that car's A-frame hazard.

I then combined these two poems together with photos of my original direction of travel and subsequent **displacement** in an opposite direction on Genesee Avenue four miles further north (see photos):

In the distance in the above photo you can see buildings that are Scripps Memorial Hospital. Both experiences were **amazing** to me, the second one especially so. That experience defies everything I/We/Science know and expect in human experience. I am not cognizant of ever having experienced a **miracle** before or since that moment. It was **dumbfounding**.

In any event, that moment has never left me or my sensibility. It has formed and influenced much of the thought in this volume. A similarly profound influence on the thought in this volume has been my readings over the past six plus decades. Everyone's reading culture will vary even as the intellectual cultural landscape is available to everyone. My readings, prior to my experience on Genesee Avenue in San Diego, California, were significantly influenced by the following authors: Sigmund Freud, Walter Kaufmann, Friedrich

Nietzsche, Bertrand Russell, William Barrett, Albert Camus, Ashley Montagu and Colin Wilson. Most of these authors were of an atheistic/agnostic persuasion. I had, of course, read many others of varying outlooks and dispositions, but these mentors were most influential in forming my mind set and philosophical convictions. Walter Kaufmann's writings, in particular, seared into my mind his disavowal of a "traditional" deity. Kaufmann was ethnically Jewish. His abhorrence of "God's" *allowance* of the holocaust and the extermination of over six million of his fellows during the Nazi death camps of World War II was forceful and compelling.

Divine Excuses (and Explanations)

Can anything make a measurable difference
to travesties suffered by vulnerable humans
when taken out of life and living
in this our only known world and reality?
Can divine excuses and explanations
change the reactions of those taken out
of their only known world and reality
when thence translated to another world
of a transcendence foreign and immaterial?
One's imagination needs to work on this
to allow Divinity the upper hand
in providing the ground-swell
and the ground-rules
to what is apropos and necessarily relevant
to human reality and human existence?
Does this require an amplified sapience?
How easily can **you** give up **your** reality?
Would God's "larger purpose" make sense to you?
What about "No" excuses or explanations?

This is a matter not easily resolved by human reason. One easily shares Kaufmann's *disbelieving*. Empty platitudes simply don't work here.

After my miracle experience I began reading the Bible in earnest––first the New Testament and then the Old. I found the Old Testament to be sometimes shocking and disturbing, especially its depiction of its venerated Deity. With the passage of time I continued to read and explore other authors. Books by Carl Jung were of significance to me.

I continued reading in the forest of doubt: Victor Stenger, Thomas Sheehan, Gregory J. Riley, Paul L. Davies, many others. Bart Ehrman was particularly influential. His book, <u>God's Problem</u>, I read five times. His reasoning I found made a lot of sense. Studies of the Book of Job in the Old Testament also made strong impressions on me. Leslie D. Weatherhead's book, <u>The Christian Agnostic</u>, was a welcome read. Additionally, I have recently read Daniel C. Maguire's book <u>Christianity Without God</u>. Its subtitle is <u>Moving beyond the Dogmas and Retrieving the Epic Moral Narrative</u>. Mr. MaGuire is a resigned Catholic priest who lost his faith in God but has held on to Christ's and the Jewish belief in a global morality of care, nurturing and human commonality, that we need to take care of one another. Excellent reasoning.

My journey through the forest of doubt (atheistic writings/culture) has been extensive and revealing. Most such reflections hold to a standard:

Faith
(isn't knowledge)

Hard headed believers are problematic:
They think their beliefs are certifiable
and fail to recognize their true nature:
Allegiance to some person or view

that may be based on religious scriptures
that have their origin in propositions
ancient perhaps are largely untestable.
Proofs for propositions require testing
to establish some form of verifiability
and must be grounded in human experiencing
that is repeatable and thus certifiable.
Without this standard one cannot claim
to **know with certainty** untold beliefs
that may be entirely fanciful and thus
not soundly socially communicable.
Personal experience is ironically confining.

This is a standard scientifically applicable to the material world we all live in. It does, however, have limitations: There is much we do not know about the human condition, and not everything can be reduced to scientific measurement. My experience on Genesee Avenue is confining by the above standard——as an expression that can be easily and readily assented to. None-the-less, I **know what I experienced**, and for me that experience has been **decisive**.

Man
(in the Wilderness)

I am a man who has lived
in the wilderness
of our intellectual culture
who, by the grace of God,
has come out of that wilderness.
I have resisted being weak
cowardly and lacking in resourcefulness
in addressing issues of alienation
mortification and self-consciousness:
I have striven to stand tall
in self-understanding and wisdom.
The journey I have been on

has brought me to this place
and this time
of enlarging awareness.

Enlarging
(awareness)

Stagnation in mental acuity
may be the destiny of some
but I believe all are called
to enlarging awareness
of the space one occupies:
Is there not time enough
to find time for exploration
of the many matters that concern you?
Enlarging one's awareness is expansive
of mind, heart and spirit
and can lead to a greater transcendence
in thought, feeling and consciousness
that can transform one's life and living
to dimensions of
unexpected exceptionalness.

Somewhere in all the doubting the heart grapples and grabs hold of hope, and that hope clambers in a slow walk to faith, faith in a Deity that may be vague in that faith's vision and clarity, but knowledgeable of that Deity's uncanny and impressive **powerfulness.**

Experiencing a miracle is the **enabler** that has helped to make this happen in me. It is the certification that one is on the right path––the **true** path.

I give you my existential ruminations.

EXISTENCE

And

ETERNITY

Meaning
(and Existence)

What gives meaning to existence?
A life of engagement and involvement
in the numerous aspects and features
of the givens of confronting reality:
Success and failure is endemic.
You are on a journey from birth to death
——quitting that excursion is not an option
if you possess a grounding
in responsible behavior and allegiance
to high principles of orientation and conduct:
Love is integral to one's existence
——love of others and love of self:
High or low, in or out, staying the course
is ultimately what it's all about.

Gift
(of Existence)

How many of us ever stop to consider
that our given existence of life is a gift?
Consider the opposite of given existence
––a state of nothingness––total nonbeing:
We can't imagine that because we exist
and live our lives as fully conscious.
And that reality is truly a gift
compared to never having ever existed.
Granted, this is an <u>interpretation</u>
of humanly existence, especially so
when one lives a miserable life
but even so one could count life a blessing
for being alive contra vacuous nothingness.
What are you making of your gift of existence?
What are your projects, your plans and your dreamings?
Where are they taking you for yourself and others?

Lights
(out)

Is it true that when we die
the lights go out forever more?
Why should we hope for ever life
when what we see and know right here
is life comes to a natural end
and doesn't waken ever again
in this our world of starts and stops?
Wishing for a future life
where everything is bright and gay
seems like a dream that falls away
soon as the day breaks clear to say
it was a fantasy of ephemeral play.
But hearts resist such dismal truth
for want of love for all they've known:
'Lights on!' echoes across the millennia!
is this we pray.

Being
(in the World)

Consider coming into existence
in the world:
If you're born into a troubled place
life could be hazardous and very fragile
with many possible deaths
dotting the landscape
––even in a most peaceful place
death could snatch you unawares
by dint of car or cancer
or multiple opportunities for violence:
One doesn't get to choose
the place of one's birthing
or the environment of one's rearing:
Is the place of one's origin
and circumstance
an unfathomable mystery?
The trajectory of one's life?

Simple
(prelude?)

Some say that this life
is a simple prelude
to what awaits us in eternity.
Well, this life is complex enough
so I would venture to say this:
This life is a **complex** prelude
to an ever greater complexity
that awaits all in eternity:
Look around you: In the sciences,
the arts, the humanities, governance,
in every phase of life––complexity!
and this must surly be a harbinger
of what awaits us in eternity:
Profound **complexity** to ever **grow** into.

Finite
(ness)

A centrally important awareness
is the realization of one's finiteness:
Defensive mechanisms operate in one
to deflect/deny this awareness
so mastering that realization
and shedding defensive mechanisms
will help to <u>liberate</u> one
to work with and against the inevitable:
You are going to die one day!
Therefore why not plan and prepare
for that inevitability?
What do you want to achieve in life?
Deciding on that will help to determine
what your hours and days will be about:
Be realistic: Plan and prepare for
your ending!

Irreconcilable (differences)

How, in Eternity, does God resolve these:
Irreconcilable differences
that occur between people?
How does peace obtain
when people are adamantly opposed
and will not be reconciled?
What is God's answer to such issues?
Is one position valued superior to another?
Does God **adjust** people?
Is that His solution?
Manipulation of people-position outlooks?
Reconciliation by mental-emotional **adjustments**?
Is there any other way? Control by God?
By fiat? God's dictatorship? Hmmm?
Does liberty, then, not exist in Eternity?

Here
(then Gone)

Everyone lives with this reality:
Alive one day, then departed
gone to death––unknown the greatest:
Do we travel to adventure
in another realm resplendent
or to a Hellish misadventure
where no respite ever chances?
Many accounts have been proffered
of a living supremely enchanted
with few of fearful dire encounters.
Life on Earth is but a testing
school of trials to firm and temper
or is it terminal, a mere ending
without future venue tending?
One does truly hope for better
none the less, we come, then vanish.

Eternal
(life)

What are the nuts and bolts
of Eternal life?
We don't possess solid details
of the life that goes on there:
Many near deathers
have given rosy pictures
of their excursions there
but nothing beyond
those brief adventures
of what transpires there.
What does it mean to live forever?
We can fill in vast many blanks
using our imaginations
but that picture is entirely fanciful
and void of real sound proofs
——thus we are left with
an invisible blank stare?

Human
(Roguishness)

Failure of imagination
failure to expand consciousness
failure to explore reality
failure to enlarge awareness
failure to be modest and humble
failure to think alternatively
failure to walk in another's shoes
failure to step outside
one's beliefs and biases
failure to entertain another's viewpoints
failure to conduct sound thinking
failure to correct arrested development
failure to practice empathy and sympathy
failure to counter inner narrowness
——these are some roguish human somethings
that are parts of human roguishness.

$\mathfrak{Major}$
$\mathfrak{(adjustment)}$

The New Testament speaks of eternal life
and makes it something to be desired:
Would anyone <u>really</u> not wish for this
and for their loved ones, especially family?
Of course, we don't know much about this
or what to expect when we're out of body
––meaning, I suppose,
we'd be something spiritual
a spiritual body, but what is that?
It is a fact that in this life and world
we are all material, biological beings
so being transformed to something non-material
would be some kind of major adjustment ...
but, if some significant life similarity
were even so given and made agreeable
and oneself and others integrated as loving
human beings sans rancors and divisions
then the question becomes:
How does that happen?

Insouciant
(ambivalence)

I'm living in my cubby-hole
strong and secure in isolation
with familiars all very common
that give me place and regular provisions
——I move around within this hole
and find myself at peace and whole
safe from external fights and foes
mindless of turmoils beyond my doors
I'm safe and secure and very happy
with this my existential condition
free from thoughts of horrible happenings
that afflict so many of my worldly neighbors:
Is this condition familiar to you
and to your warm insouciant ambivalence?
Should you be doing something about this?

Undiscovered
(country)

We know nothing of Hyper Reality,
that reality beyond Intermediate Reality
that is revealed by near death experiences
the data disclosed to those chosen exponents
of tunnels, life-reviews, illuminated figures,
of encounters with previously deceased relatives:
Those "experiences" are entirely partial
of limited scope and questionable duration
and leave one wondering what isn't revealed
that might explain the greater reality
that is never spoken of nor genuinely configured:
Various clues may be accepted from scriptures
but again those still leave us wondering
and needful of speculating beyond firm certainty.
Hyper Reality is still the "undiscovered country."

Communication
(obstacles)

There are many obstacles to communication
but the overpowering obstacle to dialectic
and the one that overrides all others
is the mental-emotional mindset
that opposes issues viewed as obdurate,
offensive, oppressive, and contemptible
to previous thought patterns and considerations
fixed in the conversant's comprehensive makeup
that demonstrates his or her resistance
to further discussion or deliberation
of subjects: A barrier arises
that announces inadmissible discussion
of a topic or topics that also declares
a closed-mindedness to further dialogue:
Such an obstacle defines the communicant
as someone unfit for higher discourse?

Higher
(discourse)

Higher discourse requires conditions
of openness, honesty and receptivity
to phenomenological professional allowance
of thoughts, ideas and considerations
for estimations and evaluations
that may arise in deliberations
of subjects, topics and various matters
that perhaps might tread upon
previously acquired mental-emotional mindsets
in the course of doing one's daily living
that may require some cautious re-evaluating
to avoid any possible brash dismissings
of possible nuggets of inspiration
and insights into possible higher illuminations.

Not to Be
(is Tragedy)

After death, after the grave
Not to Be is Tragedy
——after a long life lived
to one's approximate potential
not to Be beyond it all
is absolute, unequivocal tragedy!
To feel, to breathe, to take life in
to know the joy of Love
to share one's warmth
and know of others'
to hope, aspire and celebrate
to know that loss and gain is Life
for this to End is Tragedy:
One's heart, one's mind,
one's everything
to end, to End, is tragedy!

To Wake
(refreshed)

"Psalm 103:15-16 forthrightly observes:
"Our days on earth are like the grass
like wildflowers, we bloom and die".
"The wind blows, and we are gone––
as though we had never been here."
Compounding this is the further thought
that we will never have been there, i.e.,
the nether realms of Eternity itself!
If that is so, we'll never know
thus life will end, and pain as well:
But what a joy it might just be
to wake refreshed in Eternity
to live again, perhaps forever,
with lots to do and love eternal!

Existential
(Bad Faith)

Existential bad faith is paramount
in those that haven't learned
to **recognize** and **self-admit**
duplicities and deviousness
in dealings with all others
to own up to dishonesties
that tell the lie to smother
the truth of what one's really about
in actions with one's brothers
and sisters, indeed all others
one wants to keep confounded
about one's true intentions:
Growing to **self-insight** is key
to behaviors upright ever.

Eternity
(or not)

What do we really know about God?
His existence, character, nature, principles?
All human beings develop in a culture,
one that predisposes each to various views
—–so everyone will have a separate take,
set of opinions, varying from each other.
We do not have direct contact with God
but we do have our individual experiences
and it is from those experiences
that we do determine —–and favor—–
our individual outlooks
on the big God questions.
None will ever have absolute certainty
about those questions and conclusions
and so must wait for answers in Eternity
or not as we individually experience It **or not.**

Hallelujah (and Heartbreak)

Much of our earthly life
is hallelujah and heartbreak:
Rejoicing high and falling low
rising up and falling down
exulting keen and grieving deep
jubilating great and wallowing grave
winning grand and losing blue
and supporting all of this
is and are the human emotions
a major significance in life experience:
Beyond the head and heart
and basic to all we know
is this invariable human datum:
The soul undeniable of all experience.

Eternal
(Nada)

I am prepared to accept
eternal NADA ––eternal nothingness
if that is what there is
that awaits this wandering bark
this exile from the land
of eternal somethingness
of eternal joyous sunshine
if that is what there is
although I would prefer
that latter eternal somethingness
where life goes on eternally
that never ends in growing
into an unending future
where love does reign
most dominant.

Clouded
(emotions)

Have you let your Reason
be clouded by emotions?
Emotional fixations
can do that to you,
can supersede sound reasoning
by failures and frustrations
that cloud them out
and produce and create
angry resentments, oppositions
that drive out better judgments
on what's more important
in the larger range of sentiments:
Should your emotional life be subservient
to your overarching ethos of principles?

Swept
(clean)

What is the condition of your soul?
Does it need to be swept clean?
Will this not be its fate
when you enter into eternal life?
What will that mean? Does it seem
something like that must happen to all
who pass on through the pearly gates
into the realms of eternal life?
Perhaps it will also require much scrubbing
to clean those spots of ingrained smudging
that linger within you––long neglected
that you've overlooked or not attended
that needs such attention and remission
for your eternal entrance into the Everlasting.

Feelings
(and Words)

Which comes first: feelings or words?
Correspondence works between these two
realities in human experience
and incorporate in human reality:
The human body is feeling experience
at the initial level: feelings come first
then come words to articulate those feelings.
Human experience is existential
comes at the feeling level
which is basic to human reality.
Ideation follows what is felt
which is feeling in the initial moment:
Words are efforts to acclaim reality
and first are formed in feelings human.

Forever
(question)

What is God doing
with the daily thousands
who enter into death
with questionable, erroneous behaviors
that are ostensibly unsound
and lacking wholesome morality?
Is the Deity entirely mindful
of the incredible number of miscreants
who daily enter into Its homeland
of the eternal, everlasting forever?
What does God do to accommodate
such derelicts to their final frontier
and is there any possible
happy homeland
for their everlasting eternity?

Unforgiving
(judgmentalism)

Who is guilty of
unforgiving judmentalism?
How easy is it
to be so mischievous
as to project onto others
such harsh, nasty treatment?
Somewhere in that matrix there is
failure of thought
failure of coherence
failure of character integrity
failure of complexity awareness
failure of love and generosity
failure of wholesome spirituality!

Spiritual
(growth)

Life is a miracle to be honored
by respecting its many manifestations
of body, feelings, education, maturation
by perfecting talents, nurturing ambitions
developing skills, extending awareness
by learning to cultivate spiritual growth
that may be viewed as a culmination
of those many facets one's life acquires:
Spiritual growth is a type of pinnacle
as well as a process one might develop
to reach an end point of personal acuity
perspicacity, sensitivity, appreciation
comprehension, intelligence, penetration
of values to live and eventually die with.

Shutting Out
(insights)

Setting the ground rules
for shutting out insights begins in that region
of one's existential growth
when one makes the assumption
that one possesses superiority
in areas of knowledge acquisition:
It becomes difficult to recognize
one's arrogance and vanity
as instruments for this felony.
Learning humility and profound
self-assessment requires probity
of heart, mind and spirit
and unabated honesty devotion.

Naturalistic (Worldview)

Persons possessing scholarly aptitudes
and otherwise college educated students
who've absorbed the cultural milieu
and spirit of contemporary scientism
generally proclaim a **naturalistic worldview**
that brooks no countenance for theology
or supernaturalistic philosophies
that harbor views of an afterlife,
of gods or angels or demons:
This is the weltanschauung/worldview
that permeates the minds of many
who live in our contemporary society
imagining themselves well informed
and up-to-date on life and universe:
Do these "knowers" need a greater rigor
of inquiry into life's more obscure secrets?

Holding
(network)

Where is the holding network
that keeps us all together
that protects us from ourselves
and all our fellow inmates
in this our turbulent world
with all its various vicissitudes?
How many of us finally succumb
to the violence that surrounds us
that works to tear us asunder
from our life and our endeavors
that might promote our safety
in the network we call existence?
We need to come together
in realization of our fragility!

Heavenly
(control?)

Consider the wide variances
existing in human nature
——proclivities for behaviors
stretching to untold limits:
Now transfer that reality
to the eternal afterlife
and imagine how interactions
be conducted among individuals:
How would God arbitrate exchanges
or otherwise control individuals
to perform and function
to divine standards
that would eliminate idiosyncrasies
prohibitively undesirable
in a kingdom presumably heavenly?

Uncritical
(acceptance)

Uncritical acceptance
of words, oral or written,
is natural to youth
and easily forgiven
——but when one's grown older
and learned to think critically
there comes a time
when **truth** becomes imperative:
Critiques and analyses
of ancient scriptures
give us insights
into other scenarios:
How far dare we stray
from the natural world order?
How contrary is it to believe in miracles?
If you haven't experienced one
you likely won't accept them.

Sorrows
(of Death)

The sorrows of death are manifold
and not easily understood without experience
of life and love and permanent parting
of dear ones who leave without warning
or even with when they do escape us:
We envision the loss of those leaving
the life they will miss in departing
the care taken from us in their exiting.
A void is created in our bosoms
for the love no longer shareable in existing
with those who do journey thence from us
–– only hope and desire remain in us
for their continuance in another dimension
we cannot know nor share in this living:
We engage in this pain and vastation
all others who have ever known
such suffering.

Old
(Unconsciousness)

Before I came to be
before being born into this world
I was, I suppose, a 'not at all'
my existence ... not a 'thing'
––there was no consciousness
no self to apprehend existence
and thus not even 'old unconsciousness'
only oblivion, nada, nothingness:
Some say to this we do return
when death does come ...
eternal cessation, total nonbeing
––but I prefer to think straight otherwise
since I have felt the grace of God
and hope and trust Life will go on
and I will glow eternally ... with you
and all and everyone who ever was
or was conceived but not evolved.

Backwater (Universe)

Are we all living
in a backwater universe
where every lived event
is a merely stagnant moment
we imagine to be important
because we all suffer
from a limited and lame
sense of relevance
to a greater reality
that is beyond our scope
of comprehension and understanding?
Is that greater something
we will apprehend only
when we are dead and gone
from this our ephemeral world?
Will there be a more eventful awakening?
Stay tuned? News coming shortly?

TRUTH
and
REALITY

Acquaintance
(with the Truth)

In the thralldom of youthful guidance
specifically religion and attendant urgings
what tremendous labor it does take
to seek acquaintance with the Truth
that may lie millennia beyond that youth
and the many influences it did acquire:
Freeing oneself from false convictions
requires a devoted interest in learning
to shed the barnacles of others' believings
that were transmitted into one's being.
Acquaintance with the Truth is never easy
and does require a concerted effort
to ferret out and eventually fathom
those truths that then assume
Highest Value.

Search
(for Truth)

What is the search for truth
if not a seeking for verifications from experience
that confirm one's intellections
about those concerns
sensed most compelling
for investigation and for living
with the realities found about one:
This ultimately amounts to
a comprehensive looking into
all those matters related to
one's paramount fathoming
of what is of utmost importance
to self and others––now and forever.

Truth
(upright)

Always and all ways, truth is Truth
--some will always try to wiggle out
but always and all ways Truth will out
sooner or later with honest souls:
Striving for Truth is noble ambition
is a matter of character-integrity
of decency, humaneness,
of standing upright
of standing tall in the record of right.
Those who betray this worthy endeavor
should always be measured accurately
and recognized as either incompetent
or dangerously deviant
in human constitution:
But first comes insight
into one's ultimate morality!

Belief
(systems)

All of us are born into belief systems
sometimes one system in conflict with another
or others as the case may be
but usually one system becomes dominant
in our individual psyches
to provide some coherence and direction
in our beliefs, outlooks and affections:
A more ambitious psyche––consciousness––
will seek to question and challenge
one's inherited belief system(s)
to determine it or their validity
verifiability and inherent truth structure:
Those whose belief system(s)
don't change over time
may be guilty of negligent
truth tempering?

View
(of reality)

What is your view of reality?
Are you aware and knowledgeable
of the many forces and influences
that have worked their way on you——
dominating persons who've played roles
institutions and corporate instructions
peers and groups that have influenced you
classrooms and instructors all
——all these many who've assisted
in impressing you their views
of what reality is all about——
that is a collective set of influences
that have served you all your life
from whom you've forged
your view of reality.
Can you articulate
your vision's
View?

Cosmically
(parochial)

There is no getting around it
--we all are cosmically parochial
we live in a world of local concretes
in our minds a world of acquired specifics
each of us has a particular history
that is shared progressively with many others
our physical locations change over time
our social acquaintances do the same
our mind-sets alter variously over the years
our perspectives change with advancing age
and of course we live in a world that is local
to a solar system that is the same
in a galaxy that is one of billions
and a universe that may be one of trillions:
Fact: we are all parochial in myriad ways!

Encompassing
(ignorance)

Are we not a species enveloped
in an encompassing ignorance
that extends from our beginnings
to our present manifestations
and beyond to our future expressions
on this our increasingly bounded
planet not of our making?
Of course we are not self-created
as is our increasingly diminishing sphere
of a globe we providentially inhabit
between our yesterdays and tomorrows:
Whence have we come
and where are we going
in our staggering astounding nescience?

Evolution
(ever changing)

In all things we can see
is an ever changing evolution
that both amazes and confounds
when juxtapositions are presented
showing contemporary beliefs
——"facts" and "reasonings"——
with earlier, even ancient
facts and reasonings:
How marvelous and remarkable
the transformations we observe
in what had been we now perceive
to be so different in their accepted "forms":
We needs must attend to transformations
to embrace all "truths" we most admire?

Intelligence
(and realization)

Intelligence and realization
may not come easily unless invested
in propositions that spring from duty
to seek for truth and sound desire
for understanding sans advantage
and questionable leverage of some other
directive or position not truly relevant
to the highest truths one is seeking:
Sincerity of purpose is a learning
that may take time and proficient patience
to cultivate and acquire by sensible schooling
the mind, heart and selfless passions
to learn to know what may be thwarted
by lesser concerns for what is highest.

Quest
(for Self-Definition)

Who does not engage in
the quest for self definition?
That quest is inevitable
in the process of human growth
and one's interaction with culture
with one's education and environment
and the many forces and influences
that present themselves
to the individual person:
The need for finding a profession
or occupation for making a living
and the assessment of one's qualities
talents and abilities––all pool into
the quest that produces self definition:
What one becomes is the answer
to self definition and its quest.

Implacable
(death)

The reality of life
is implacable death
that necessarily awaits one
somewhere, sometime
which, with awareness,
may catapult one
to extraordinary effort
in the doing of one's life:
One needs to discover
what one loves in life
and then to pursue that
to one's fullest ability
to the end that reality
acknowledges one's living.

Extraordinarily
(speculative?)

Perhaps you feel compelled to exclaim
that my thoughts are extraordinarily speculative
and I could counter 'You might be right'
but, on the other hand, what I've to say
is grounded in some personal experience
that isn't common, or so I've seen,
by observing others who make no claims
to having experienced a bona fide miracle
that makes a difference in the scheme of things:
I spin my thoughts for you to consider
and articulate my grasp of my experiences
to the end that you may make comparisons
and ultimately decide, just for yourself,
where truth chips fall and finally lay.

Social
(juggernaut)

My personal experiences
are not your personal experiences:
Why should you believe
one of my personal experiences
especially an extraordinary one
when you've never had it
unless you thoroughly trust me
and know I don't speak fictions?
This is a juggernaut in social camaraderie
especially when that personal experience
is entirely private without evidence
that can be socially shared
thus dis-enabling social assent
and profound communal concurrence?

Concrete
(experiences)

What are those concrete experiences
that help to define you
that make you the person you are?
Experiences form the core, the nucleus,
of every person's self-identity
and profoundly contribute to one's growth
——intellectual, emotional and spiritual——
that continues throughout one's life:
For some those experiences are nebulous
even forgotten, but were concrete
in the formation of one's psyche——
and they continue to influence
one's thinking and behaviors
and are the tsunami of self-identity:
Can you name those experiences
and make them explicit
in your contemplations?

Proclivities
(and Fixations)

Don't we all inevitably
come to conclusions of our own making
that depend on our reasonings
our experiencing and our dreaming
that fit with our dispositions
to believe and to imagine
what is real, what is possible
what is finally acceptable
to our proclivities and fixations?
The universe of our beliefs
is bound to these determinants
that settle in our thinking
making us either inflexible in our natures
or open, unbiased and growing.

Examine
(the Evidence)

Have you started out just to believe
to study doctrines to bolster faith
or have you seriously exerted yourself
to **examine the evidence** pro and con
on the issues you seek to determine
whether true or false, right or wrong?
Your original orientation is entirely crucial
and can be forgiven if blighted by youth
and its concomitant limited discernment
of what is sound comprehensive judgment
of all those variables to be considered
in your evaluation of those matters:
Learning to seek always for the truth
may require counseling of a higher order
of intelligence and realization.

Easy
(believing)

Unfortunately, in this modern age,
we must guard against *easy believing*
that was learned simply by osmosis
in our infancy and youthfulness:
Knowledge of complex issues
now surrounds us
if we are attentive and studious
and responsible earnest learners.
What is easy to believe
may be fraught with somber hazards
of delinquent focus-concentration
that, perhaps on <u>investigation</u>,
proves to be dubious, even fallacious,
showing thus a backward immaturity
that would embarrass around the learned.

Spiritual
(beings)

We are all spiritual beings
who need to get in touch
with our existential experiences
to fully fathom our marvelous
individual natures
their complexities of value
of awakening thoughts and emotions
of inter-connectedness
with our spacious and towering
breadths and depths of meaning
that translates and transposes us
one to another in a universe
of life and feeling and wonderment
that is our sphinx-like
all encompassing reality.

Infused
(thinking)

Have you ever experienced automatic writing
or had ideas pop into your mind
and wondered how on earth they happened?
Those experiences are a reality
and come from a source most don't recognize:
Providers on the Other Side who are adept
at supplying to us without our being
conscious of their transmissions
perhaps initially or even ever
but come they do as many have marveled
and some know emphatically what is happening:
We may never know the 'why' of such
but can know this: Our subconscious minds
are conduits for many wondrous offerings
that may also be considered: Gifts!

𝕰𝖒𝖔𝖙𝖎𝖔𝖓𝖆𝖑
(𝖉𝖎𝖘𝖙𝖆𝖓𝖈𝖊)

How many people can you count—–
family members or persons of acquaintance
that between the two of you there exists
something quite extraordinarily common:
The fact of your being emotionally distant?
We often live our lives in such fashion
and measure our relationships inconsequentially
by failing to promote recognition accord
or emotional bonding with any frequency:
We may keep some in close correspondence
while many others with little attention
and thus such lack of significant rapport
renders that relationship as truly nominal
—–remote and devoid of **feeling entreaty**.
Emotional distance is a pervasive norm.

Something
(amiss?)

In the deep recesses of your Soul,
your Spirit, your Memory
there must be love for all——
for Mother, Father and Siblings
for those you grew up with
for neighbors and community
for the nation of your rearing
for the world you were born into
for blue skies and green grass
for trees and bees and flowers
for all of these and more
Love bathed you most exquisite:
If you cannot find this love in you,
do you suppose there is
something amiss in you?

Self
(understanding)

Isn't it so very amazing
that presumably educated persons
can fail to truly know themselves
——that nexus of those esemplastic
needs and motives and dire intentions
that bounce about within themselves
when tests arrive presenting challenges
profoundly unexpected or unwanted?
Isn't a truly liberated/liberal person
sage to a sense of science
about the world within and out
that harkens one to cautious treading
when dealing with the great unknowable
that surrounds us all in our interiors
and to a modest genuine unknowing?

Thinking
(critically)

How often are we asked
to eschew thinking critically?
Many think criticism is offensive
avoid it as disagreeable
find it to be objectionable
and dodge its positive relevance
in plumbing issues of complexity
that require intellectual discernment
and careful penetrating discipline:
Isn't it quite amazing
that in our culture generally
even 'educated' persons
can regard thinking critically
to be socially unacceptable?
Are such persons truly learned?

Conditioned
(responsiveness)

There is only one answer
to conditioned responsiveness
when it comes to religion
philosophy and world outlooks:
Extensive study with intensive attention
to the voluminous propositions
that are pervasively promulgated.
One should also check within
to observe one's addictedness
to positions ingrained in one's psyche
from earliest indoctrinating:
Devotion and adherence
to standards of truth and convictioning
is the only reliance available
for deciding what is right and true.

Laboring
(over God)

I've been laboring over God
since my late teens
when I decided then
to dismiss the whole thing
––threw the baby out
with the bath water––
then experienced some shattering
episodes of personal torments
and reversed my course
some twenty years later:
I'm still laboring now
and have found no rest
from my tireless labors:
Does God enjoy being a mystery?

𝕱athoming
(emotions)

It is apparent to me from my experiences
that understanding and fathoming emotions
is intricately important to human wholeness
and living a full and enriching life:
It is inevitable that one **feels** in life
and pressures may bear on their suppression
or even, at worse, on their repression
which most empathically can cause divisions
within one's psyche and interior operations:
Conflicts, of course, are going to happen
but freedom from interior divisions
and psychosomatic distress/disorders
will make for a more wholesome demeanor
and interactions with life's many adventures.

Emotion
(as Instrument)

Have you ever noticed
how stimuli affect you
––first your feelings, your emotions
then your thinking––inspirations
leading you to plans and actions
that expand upon emotions
and the stimuli you've experienced?
As this plays out
one begins to see
one's emotions as an instrument
that oft gets played upon
by stimuli surrounding one:
Should one play one's emotional instrument
to effect one's better thinking?

Sufficiently
(developed)

Insight, knowledge and wisdom
require one to be sufficiently developed
in learning, thought and reflection
to appreciate mysteries inherent in existence:
All today stand on the shoulders
of past generations and cultural developments
that can inform and admonish some among us
of what was previously fathomed
and highly wrought for attentive successors:
We might apply ourselves to that that was wrought
and insure that we be sufficiently developed
if we would appreciate our generous inheritance
in order to apply that inheritance to current endeavors
that give honor and reverence
to what we have been bestowed.
What our forefathers have given us
deserves respect, reverence and honor
however misguided they may themselves have been
in our current sense of enlightenment
——for they stood on their forefathers shoulders
as we surely do in our own time.

Great Drama
(of Existence)

Immersed in the business of living
we barely cognize the marvelous story
of our existence, its great drama
that totally surrounds us every minute:
We can see it in stories of adventure
in movies of the same we marvel at
in the lives of public figures, celebrities
of outstanding athletes, political personages
and in many remarkable people about us:
How often, though, do we recognize truly
the pace and progress of our own living
its depths and thrusts
toward higher expansions
of greater awareness
and material advancements
of compounding love
and enlarging community?
The drama of life is greatest in spirit
in the inner workings of
our individual merits.

𝔇ifferent
(realities)

Lo and behold—–think awakening to
consideration of significant departure:
People live in different realities
in their heads and emotional chambers
and often because of this
compassion and empathy
are severely negated:
Convivial communication is often truncated
when headstrong allegiances are asserted
when views and opinions are acknowledged
that serve to separate and divide
civil communion among human co-habitants:
Backtracking on one's given convictions
is rarely conceived of or never considered
in a comparative light of illumination.

Compatible
(spirit)

What is a compatible spirit?
Someone who is willing and desires
to entwine agreeably with another
who is capable of blending harmoniously
with another's constitution and complexity
who finds it easy to get along well
with another's views and outlooks
who seeks to be in agreement
with another's ambitions
and sentiments
who strives to achieve congruence
with another's path and projections in life
and who also seeks the same
from those others who surround her
and willingly seek to please her **in kind**.

Deep-seated (tendencies)

When was the last time
or, in fact, anytime
when you reflected on
your **deep-seated tendencies**?
Curiously, every one has these
––they make for rigid determinants
in one's world of thought
of reflection on those issues
that occupy (or don't) one's imagination
and **dispositions** toward many
and numerous ultimate considerations:
Why there is something rather than nothing,
where God came from, yourself,
and the nexus of reality surrounding you?

Mind
(reach)

What is the reach of your mind?
Do you spend all your days
reaching for wealth
for fame and glory
for love and affection
for self-aggrandizement?
What will your legacy be?
Do you seek to serve others
in some significant capacity
to enable their advancement
in self-understanding enrichment
to connect others
to a greater community
with themselves and their loved ones
who came before, who'll come after?
Is giving back important
in your mental horizon?
What is most important
for you to mentally reach for?

Silence
(is Golden?)

Silence is Golden? Silence is Selfish!
Good manners and taste
demand responsiveness!
What is behind the motive of silence?
Judgmentalness, fear and substantial laziness
with a strong dash of selfishness thrown in:
Judgmental because of too swift opinionating
fear because of worried anticipation
one may be hooked into some answerability
and laziness because of some effort required
when one is accustomed to no special exertion
——all of which spell out a total selfishness
which is a characterizing of real personage:
So silence is Golden for this sort of person
who clambers behind a blind self-deception
and a truly thoroughgoing
authentic shallowness!

Beloved
(community)

Heaven must surely be
a *beloved community*
where every single member
has learned and practices
loving behaviors toward all others
for if not so
we'd be back here
in our divisive world
where angry disagreements
congest out relationships
and our courts
where violence and wars
propagate promiscuously
and dangers lurk
in unseen corners.

GOD, RELIGION

and

the SUPERNATURAL

Thoughts
(about God?)

I do not know God.
Statements about God beggar convictioning.
Who among us knows anything about God?
How is it possible to know God?
Who can speak with authority about God?
Articulations about God may evolve from scriptures.
Faith in scriptures may inspire belief in God.
Positive propositions about God cannot be tested.
Does that mean such propositions are invalid?
God's existence cannot be proven or disproven.
Inferences about God may warrant reflection.
Wishful thinking accumulates around ideas of God.
God seems to prefer being unavailable to mankind.
Does this provoke some to generate aspirations?
Intense spiritual adventuring into speculations?
Do many turn away because of God being unavailable?
Is God in any sense 'friendly' toward mankind?
Is God in any sense unfriendly as well?
How can God be 'love' in light of the many
negative things/happenings that occur incessantly
to people?

Straight
(talk)

Do you suppose we will ever
get straight talk from God
when we clearly do not
get such talk from Him now?
Why did this or that happen,
why did this or that not happen?
I've never received such answers
——have you? Have you never ever?
Should I thus be ruling out
so many questions of God,
or even ever expect
straight answers fairly from Him?
What lies behind God's silence,
His refusal to give **any** answers?
Does God ever answer
with **transparency**?
Is this silence all that Golden?

Any
(wonder?)

Is it any wonder
that so many wonder
about the **silence** of God?
Not providing answers
raises serious questions
about His utmost verity
as well His sound sincerity!
We are simply left alone
to puzzle over His nature,
His mystery and His loving
--if we can truly believe that:
This is a state of affairs
historical-ancient in its scope
that confounds real thinking minds.

Unobservable
(entity)

God is an unobservable entity
that innumerable people do protest
is real and to be highly regarded
as answering prayers
and giving mankind rules to live by
and otherwise as a fount of wisdom
as scriptures record——or to be feared
for placing humanity in the crosshairs
of directives to be obeyed, or if defied
to suffer consequences
of eternal punishment
in an everlasting pit
of inconceivable torment
as justly served for said defiance:
Why has God so chosen to mystify us (?)
concludes in the issue of
individual choices.

Mind
(of God)

The Mind of God is incomprehensible:
Regardless of scriptures
no one can know
what is inaccessible
to human imagination:
Savants can surmise
Popes can pontificate
Magicians can mesmerize
but nobody **knows**
the incomprehensible
Mind of God:
One can only hope for
God's justice and mercy.

Always
(in the wrong?)

Have not many said:
"In the presence of God
we are always in the wrong"?
That is a fundamentalist position.
Many Christians seek to be perfect
or consciously strive for the same:
Only God can make one perfect
by His grace––and nothing else?
All are lost without His acceptance
and admission into His heavenly realm?
What constitutes winning His grace?
Do you accept you are not perfect?
What will win His redemption?
Does this give us much to do
and think about?

Divine Power
(and Panic Disorder)

Sadly, I hold it to be true
that God exercises the power
to create 'panic disorder' in humans
for I have experienced that affliction
on multiple occasions in my life
––all in my thirties––
that resulted in three hospitalizations
in facilities for the psychologically disturbed:
I was able to leave those lodgings
each after two weeks of 'treatment':
Indeed, my behaviors were altered
progressively through those experiences
and I have never forgotten
the source of their origin: God.
Not **from** me but **through** me!

Genuine
(and Disinterested)

What could it possibly mean to have
a genuine and disinterested devotion to God
when God is intimately and essentially unknowable
at least for the vast majority of mankind
and this individual scribbler and speculator
on the divine attributes that call for devotion?
Must we assume that God possesses
those ultimate traits and greatest attributes
we humans can imagine for such a being:
Uttermost goodness, integrity, love,
justice, virtue, carefulness, care,
eternal tolerance, inexplicable power, creativity?
Is it probable that we assume too much
in our human ignorance and unknowability?
Was Job a genius in his human devotion?

Above
(human standards)

According to the Book of Job,
one of the Old Testament tomes,
God is evidently above justice
and can do whatever He pleases:
Therefore human justice doesn't apply
and can't be calculated in appraising God
and, furthermore, any such standard
that we humans can imagine
stands remotely below conceptions of God:
This truly removes God from human knowing
and creates Him a mystery beyond human fathoming
but doesn't release us from human morality
and from observing and obeying
human standards of justice
and human decency.

Divine (Indifference)

How long does one labor
under the influence
of Divine Indifference
before one loses
everlasting faith
in God's love?
Glorious hyperboles
––gross exaggerations––
of God's love
for mortal man
must needs encompass
all the horrors
and tribulations
humans have endured
throughout the ages
of human history
and contemporary
realities.

God's
(Absenteeism)

Christian theorists proclaim God
His existence in ruling mankind
making Him divine and entirely necessary
to human morality and humane behaviors
––He sets the standards the Bible says
that must regulate all human relations
and levels the playing field in human interactions
in human enterprises and social intercourses:
But where is God but in the scriptures
His presence in society a total mystery
reliance upon Him a matter of acceptance
in a dismal light of opaque structures
of thought and faith and blind adherence
without His hand or finger forbearing
His actual appearance in human endeavors?:
Does not His absenteeism provoke dissensions?
Being touched by God is **routinely** wanting.

Divine (Detachment)

I am not equipped
to fathom the mystery
that surrounds God's behaviors
and I know that I join
many other humans
in this unhappy reality
to fathom the depths
of incomprehensible evils
that occur in this world
and in innumerable lives:
That incredible disasters
occur in human lives
I cannot account for
nor condone Divine detachment.

God's
(love)

Where is God's love
when women are raped
when children are murdered
when millions are decimated
by gas or slaughtering
by the current pandemic
by senseless indifferences
nations portend to 'others'
as in the Middle East?
Consider the countless lives
that have been 'given up'
over untold eons of time
in human history . . . ?
What do those losses tell us
but that we're on our own
in the vast emptiness
of God's love?

Allowance
(is Responsibility)

Those who proclaim
that God does no Evil
but allows Evil to occur
are caught in contradiction:
Allowance is Responsibility!
The difference between
allowance and responsibility
is subtle and severe:
Allowance of Evil
is **participation** in Evil
by virtue of not prohibiting
or nullifying its occurrence.
Looking on Evil with allowance
shows indiscriminate permission
which beggars higher virtue
that is absence of righteousness.

Choosing
(to do Nothing)

Now, correct me if I'm mistaken,
but if you allow something to happen
something that is destructive to another
one that you are in full observance of
and are able to prevent from happening
––and you **choose** to do nothing––
are you not then responsible
for allowing that evil to happen?
Therefore, is not allowance responsibility?
So what, then, is God's position here?
Has not God **chosen** to stay 'hands off'?
Is there, therefore, responsibility for negatives
that occur on a regular basis to humanity?
Tell me what exonerates God from this scenario?
Where is God when such things happen?

God's
(Inaction)

What are we to make
of God's inaction
in perilous circumstances
people find themselves in?
Might one ask:
Where is His love
and does inaction count
for His failure to love?
We are presented here
with a timeless dilemma:
Believers makes excuses
disbelievers find fault
and the mystery remains
to go forever unanswered.

Corona (virus)

So you want to believe
that God is great, that He's loving
and wants the best for all creation
that He is mindful of each individual
human person who struggles forward
that He is the author of everything
and by definition incapable of evil:
Okay, so those of you who take that position
might apply your thinking to terminal matters
such as the lethal coronavirus killings
that create **unimaginable** sufferings
to those afflicted and those left losing
their cherished loved ones who do perish:
What in the name of God is He doing?
Does God have a problem with His loving?
Is there a problem with such
happy propositions?

Religious
(beliefs)

Religious beliefs are a function
of family encouragements
and community cohesions
that may be broken from
by concentrated study
and existential discomforts
with ideations found inconvenient
with hormonal inclinations
experiential discoveries
intellectual disagreements:
The search for truth
should be forthright and honest
not invested in personal comforts
or social conforming
for self-seeking benefits.

Upright
(conscience)

What must one make of
absurdities and contradictions
one finds in the Bible
and the apparent confusions
about its almighty God?
The Bible is a complex
encyclopedic jigsaw puzzle
that gives much food for thought
but finally must be absolved
of offering highest truth
in favor of sound reasoning:
Each must seek for truth
inside one's self, and practice
that which is highest
in one's upright,
honorable conscience.

Christian
(message)

The Christian message
is flawed in many ways:
Christ thought he'd be returning
as the Son of Man––and soon
but 2,000 years have now passed
and we haven't seen sight of Him!
He also taught an eternal Hell
that doesn't easily square
with human comprehension:
––His saving instruction
was a message of love
that many human beings
have yet to follow!
The overall message
needs some retooling?

Religious
(rationalizations)

What must we make of religious rationalizations?
We stand apart, many centuries now,
from conceptions enthroned in ancient verses,
tomes and scriptures since claimed from Divinity
--its abiding tidings for all of humanity:
Our many religions make claims for authority
and resent inquiries that challenge their assertions
——but numerous researches have raised many counters
to the factual bases of claims to sobriety!
We must ask ourselves, thoughtfully,
of lurking mythologies lingering in language
that beg for verification and certitude:
Ruminative minds are piercingly called for
to ferret out genuine truths from fictions.

Cinders
(and Ashes)

Consider yourself dead and resurrected
as a spiritual being in a Heavenly realm
but still retaining your likes and dislikes
your propensity for lies and dis-ingenuity:
Your author and judge will be observing you
and weighing your regard for every other
in that environment of glorious penetration
of your mind and heart and cantankerous leanings:
What do you do? Justify your propensities
and foul the region of your self's occupation
or do you take shame for your many shortcomings
and miserable uncharitableness unto others?
There will be no recourse for coarse mis-adventuring
—— judgment will rain on you like **cinders and ashes**?

Obeying
(God)

What does it mean to obey God?
Presumably to practice righteousness
which is to say behaving well
avoiding every form of evil
being nice, being good,
being considerate of others
serving them and one's self
with conscientious empathy and compassion
avoiding resentfulness when offended
thinking positively through thick and thin
refusing to let animosities fester
in one's mind and one's heart
moving agreeably with helpfulness
practicing love in every action
eschewing selfishness always
being ever hopeful and stalwart:
Is this then obeying God?

Wholesale
(inventions)

One must always be wary
of wholesale inventions
that claim authenticity
and indubitable authority
to highest truth and certification
of living reality and spiritual honesty:
What must one do?
Investigate **origins** and **propositions**
that get dispensed to gullible ears
with trappings of verification
and voluminous documentations
camouflaging **speciosity**.
Wolves in sheep's clothings
make for formidable opponents:
Christ warned of such posturing.

Impenetrable
(mysteries)

There are impenetrable mysteries
that we can never hope to solve:
One of these is the origin of God
——if you're not willing to subscribe
to the cryptic "always was and will be"
proposition that is tricky and delusive.
Another is the origin of the Big Bang
which offers the impervious enigma
of how to get behind/before that conundrum.
Science has indeed resolved
many mysteries confronting our ancestors
but cannot answer multiple questions
apropos particulars of human history
that are always, forever lost to us.
Another: Why is there something
rather than nothing?

Dismissing
(God)

It is problematic and likely erroneous
to dismiss God 'out of hand'
and even after scrupulous study:
We are a species launched in darkness
about our origins in the universe
and the wherefores of existence:
Is it not far too easy
to assimilate 'knowledge'
far exceeding us
about a deity masked in mysteries
we are not intended to uncover?
Complex reality shadows mysteries
advocating and suggesting
wonders we can barely fathom:
God is asking us to quiver
in a dimness unforgiving?

Supernatural (intervention)

What is your experience of
supernatural intervention?
Have you had such experience
sans a contrived interpretation,
one designed to impress
your religious neighbors?
A real and believable experience
would probably be dumbfounding
and leave you with many questions
that might go begging for answers
or, then again, you may never
even suspect such an action
until some maturity makes it seem
quite notable and credible.
Were laws of nature broken?
Was coincidence a salient factor?
Synchronicity?

Eternal
(extinction)

If eternal nothingness is our fate
there is nothing to be said
for there would be no consciousness
no mind, no will, a total nothingness
without form or color, no sensations
not even blackness, bleak and dreary
absolute non-being, complete emptiness
such the state of eternal extinction.
Is this easy for us to accept?
Many have assumed this is our fate
once we've passed on through this world
this life of color, hope and expectations
but near-death experiencers tell us differently
give us HOPE for an eternal somethingness!

Gift
(of Eternal Existence)

Give consideration to this possibility:
The Gift of Eternal Existence.
We cannot fathom such a reality
though religion speaks of eternal life.
If we assume such life would be mostly pleasant
then it would be a **Divine Gift**
incomprehensible in its magnitude
and entirely dumbfounding as a given:
Why should such a gift be given
to fallible, imperfect, faulty humans?
One can only reasonably imagine
a Cosmic, Loving, Caring Progenitor
to account for such a gift as that
––no other answer would make any sense!
And how improbably is one so deserving?
Even one's temporal life is a gift!

Beauty Calls Us
(to God?)

I haven't known God
but I have known beauty
in a woman's face and figure
in lovely, exhilarating music
in epic dramas of love and war
in paintings that captivate and mystify
in poetry and in literature
in scenes of nature rhapsodic
in the faces of little children
in the streets of my hometowns
in the colors and shapes of automobiles
in grasses and trees riotously colorful
in blossoming flowers and in bees
in all of nature: Is this then Divine?
All this is what is higher
and calls us to the Highest?

Author
(of All)

If God is the Author
of all that we know
––the world that surrounds us
the starry night sky
the universe outside us
what a marvelous Creator
––the beautiful blue sky
green grass and trees
the people that we love
all we cherish––from Above
we've much to be thankful for
––the gift of our lives
our joys, delights, our dreams
if God is the Author of All!

God
(and Creativity)

Whence comes human creativity
that moves toward the Transcendent?
In youth is it not inexplicable
that someone so young
could be so accomplished
and miles beyond the rest
of lagging humanity?
Is not the human brain a conduit
for celestial transmissions
that promote and advance
the inestimable in human reckoning
that dumbfounds common witnessing?
Who could be the provider of such giftedness
but the creator of such creativity: God.?

Human
(conduits)

Looking around at the world as I do
and looking at human creativity
do you not see that we are conduits
that our creativity come from a Source
a Source that is higher than our individual selves
a Source that harkens to and from God?
Human creativity is endlessly marvelous
and draws upon an Infinite Well
a Well and a Source that fully exceeds us
that sparingly pours itself lightly upon us
into our creativity that fully exceeds us
individually and collectively ... and does lead us
to recognize we are each human conduits
that comes from that which is entirely Above us.

Negative
(solutions)

There are no solutions
to the ironies of existence
to the tragedies afflicting mankind
in its daily exercises/endeavors:
Belief in a loving God
may give comfort to many
but positive answers to 'why'
cannot be satisfactorily given.
There exists an infinity of queries
about occurrences that do damage
and explanations of God's oversight
beggar convincing convictioning:
Proclaiming that 'God is love'
is no answer
to profound devastationing.
Do we need to refigure
God's high holiness?

Loving
(God)

How does one show love to God?
God is not available to us
is presumably not physically material
therefore not visually viewable
thus is alien to us . . . .
But Jesus says that we must love Him
with mind and heart and every fiber
of our physical material beings:
What is thus accessible to us?
Scripture gives us *behavioral injunctions*
we may measure variously up to them
if we're inclined to march thus to them
and this is how we show love to Him:
In *willing conformity* love is given Him?

SELF

and

OTHERS

Conceptual
(framework)

What is my conceptual framework?
It is based upon a personal experience
that is not subject to scientific verification
and could easily be dismissed by skeptics:
In August of 1979 I experienced
a reversal of traveling in San Diego:
This occurred after going to confession
at Our Mother of Confidence Catholic Church.
Subsequently, I was numinously directed
to Jesus Christ as **the** source of judgment.
I have labored over those experiences
and have contemplated doubts and misgivings:
My limitations and failures are numerous
but my hope is a future in Eternal Life.

Struck
(by Lightning)

I was once struck by lightning
——not the literal atmospheric lightning
but the atmospheric *spiritual* lightning
that subsequently affected me profoundly
and helped to significantly re-organize my life:
Through the decade of the 1970s
I experienced three traumatic afflictions
that sent me reeling into hospitalizations
each lasting for two restoring weeks
and sobering returns to psychic normalcy:
With the last hospitalization I heard a Voice
that frightened me into a serious mending
of my waywardness and obdurate unbelief:
Shortly thereafter I went to Confession
and then was struck with spiritual lightning:
On Genesee Avenue in San Diego——
I went from heading South to treading North
traversing four miles in under three seconds
and Startling Illumination:
Only God could engineer such Astonishment!
Produce in me a bolting transformation.

Original
(innocence)

Are all of us born
into original innocence
free of all sin and miscreance?
——or is there some stain
that lurks within us
that impels us to deeds
that partake of the shadowy
side of living and doing
that results in misfortune
for one's self and others?
As children we think
of ourselves as innocent
but living and growing
bring us up to the grasping
of things we have done
that fall short of innocence
and prove our naivete
of ourselves as innocents.

Disabused
(of Ignorance)

The net effect of my uncanny experience
of traversing a reversal of my traveling
a momentous four miles in a mere three seconds
in August of 1979 in San Diego, California
on Genesee Avenue of an evening
following confession at
Our Mother of Confidence Catholic Church
will never leave me for remembering
that my conception that God did not exist
was totally shattered and effectively dismantled
and left me believing that God could so manifest
a remarkable turnaround of the natural order
and leave me imagining He could accomplish
such astounding a feat that even a soul
could experience sensations out of body
and be pleasured and pained
at His august discretion:
Such was my fathoming
of this miraculous proficiency!

Deep
(imperfections)

You probably have never considered
what is basic to human nature
because most of us are conditioned
to be tolerant and overlooking
of the deep imperfections in others
as in ourselves **most decidedly**
and this can readily be ascertained
with a little vigorous effort:
Follow yourself closely
over a given stretch of time
––making notes while you go––
and you will soon easily discover
what is going on within you:
Deep imperfections
that also characterize others.

Experiential
(reality)

What I experienced in August of 1979
on Genesse Avenue in San Diego, CA
was bona fide **experiential reality**
that I'll never be talked out of:
It was no hallucination
no imagined figment
no mental aberration
no drug induced foolishness
it was the real thing––a **miracle**
and a **message** to my person:
That God, the Supernatural, was real
possessed of powers beyond this world
able to move my moving car instantaneously
four miles in an opposite direction
than I was headed––and strikingly
remarkably conspicuously astoundingly
speechlessly stupefyingly dumbfounding!
(For twenty years [20] I had been an atheist.)

How Do You
(Read?)

How do you read?
Do you read with naive gullibility
do you read with unthinking sympathy
do you read with listless sensitivity
do you read with faulty sensibility
or do you read with a careful eye
and careful thought to what's before you
measuring aptly what's presented you
to the end you might evaluate
weigh and judge on every particular
and the overall sense of perspective
of the author's calculated advancing?
Do be cautious of what's before you
to the end you're not too easily persuaded.

Admonishment
(Warning)

Punishment for sin:
I know the Bible teaches this
especially in the Old Testament
forcefully so in the New as well
and I know that today many educated believe
that such punishment no longer applies
——but I have experienced it
so I know it is real
and is sometimes addressed
to those in need
of such enlightenment:
Perhaps God administers punishment
as a necessary correction
——a *palliative* if you will——
for those requiring **admonishment**
For me it was a **warning**!

Quick
(judgment)

Are you inclined to make quick judgments
on matters you are disinclined to
when presented with circumstantial evidence
leaning in a direction you're opposed to?
Do you bring a heavily weighted suitcase
of prejudice to your impatient hearing
on such matters you're opposed to
from your extensive experience background?
Does your considerable regard for self(esteem)
propel you to alacritous mustering out
of propositions you find to be disagreeable
based on your august knowledge acquisition?
Should you consider yourself above reproach
for your superior superciliousness?
Should you slow down and be more reflective?
Less judgmental, less imperious?

GOD
(Third Person)

Something remarkable entered my awareness
when I sought the help of an Exorcist:
A priest of the Catholic Church
suggested to me
a thought I had never imagined:
That my personal afflictions
I believed the work of a demon
may have in fact been
the work of the Holy Spirit:
Such had never crossed my mind!
What I had thought was evil incarnate
that had given me **extraordinary** stress
——had driven me to psychiatric hospitalizations
was the work of God the Third Person! ...?

Unsound
(relationship)

What is it that constitutes
an unsound relationship?
A lack of openness and honesty
some form of gamesmanship
a need to be **one up** on the other
to wax superior and aloof
failure to be wholesomely sincere
withholding truthfulness
from the other
the inability to be readily clean
and clear in one's disclosures
indecisiveness in reciprocal sharing
ultimately a void of kindness
and authenticity in the present
a coy evasiveness, obliquity
of character and heartfelt good will
inconstancy of sound intentions
ignorance of one's own true advantage
in leveling the soul of humility
refusal to speak the unsaid
failure of acquaintance with one's shadow
inconsistency of motivation
immaturity of soulfulness.

Close
(to the Vest)

Emphatically, most of my poemographs
are written close to the vest
which is to say from my personal interior
or, in other words, from personal experiences
––from my mind, heart and spirit
––from my lived experiences in this world
and not just from my head or heart
or from any frivolous imaginings
that I try to avoid with all seriousness
because I want to be taken seriously
and most definitely as **authentic**
as true to nature and human reality:
I want to be believed and believable
which is what I take to be writing
"Close to the Vest"!

Clique's
(constructs)

Behind one's back
and out of sight
what words are shared
what gossip passed
how little truth
compassion's facts
when old acquaintances
plot out false tracks
and give no thoughts
to subject's plight
to give conversants
corrective sights
and qualifying truths
that set scores right?

Inner
(therapist)

At my advanced age of eighty (80)
I look back to observe my experiences
and remark that I needed extensive therapy
for my inner confusions about life and existence
about religion, sexuality, ambitions and limitations:
I became interested in psychology and philosophy
in literature, anthropology, and human history
and eventually in genealogy and a future afterlife:
I was loaded with guilts and confused ambitions
and needed therapy that I couldn't afford:
What happened in this matrix of interests and studies
and inner reflections on these many diverse interests
was that I became my own inner therapist
that has given me guidance throughout my life:
In all I've been fortunate in negotiating life's perils.

Breaking through (Another's consciousness)

Breaking through another's consciousness
that has determined to be impenetrable
is like drilling
for gold
in a hard rock candy mountain
where no gold exists
and no wealth can be extracted.
The sad part of this is
that one's love is abrogated
where the mind, heart and spirit
the desire, will and emotion
the intellect and the wisdom
are bereft of spirituality
to be ever known, loved or cherished
by the seeker of such fortune.

Spirit
(Guide)

I'm aware that in my thinking
I've been influenced and guided by
the conflux in that thinking
and my ultimate acceptance of
the possibly more challenging alternative
and my submission to
the more correct, honest and responsible
direction that thinking guided me:
Is that indication of a Spirit Guide
that has prevailed upon me
to take the better, more responsible course
in my behavior and my outlooks?
My awareness of such a Spirit Guide
is thus remote and not yet interpersonal:
I am locked into my mental exertions
—— will a personal encounter ever follow?
Who could possibly be my Spirit Guide?

Perpetual Existence
(in a Cave)

How long have you lived
in that cave of your making
the one that is cloistered
unkempt and oppressive
that doesn't encourage
friendly visits from others
who might be curious
to know more about you
but are discouraged
by the limited access
you avail to those others
and the needless barriers
you present to those others
for expanded consciousness?

Imperfect
(life)

My life has been imperfect
and yes, I know, most lives are
——mine has had its own contours
with its share of misbehaviors
of ups and downs, gains and losses
and yet I've persevered
because it's natural so to do
and quitting's not my dna
——I've wished some things
had been graciously different
have wondered at life's causes
but life is always a mixed affair
that's never totally in one's control:
Finally, I've sought for what is higher.

Come out!
(Come out!)

How long will you go on
"limping on both legs"
and operating from that cave
where you've buried your heart?
Come out! Come out!
Let the light astound you
reflect on your notions
your precious conceptions
you believe to be true
that may be erroneous
that reveal you are living
an unexamined life:
Enlarge your awareness
––start asking hard questions!

Compulsion
(to Write)

The compulsion to write
hasn't run in my families
though my mother wrote poetry
and I've published a book
of poemographs––*Rogues' Gallery*
and a Master's Thesis
on Ernest Hemingway's
Nick Adams short stories:
I admire those prolific
in their use of the pen
––can only wish I were gifted
in the art of invention/disclosure
more than I've been or will be:
The compulsion to write
has been modest within me.

Busting
(out)

When are you going to
bust out of that straight jacket
you've placed yourself in
––the one that is lily white
with tight fitting symmetrical buttons
and controlling zippers
that configure your arms
to arrested movements
and confines your mind
your heart and your spirit
to a narrowed vision
of the entirely possible
and bubblingly bountiful?

Pursuit
(of Individuality)

When I was younger, ages 20 to 50,
my pursuit of individuality
was strong within me
and even today those drives
remain in my consciousness
––but I no longer *act* on them
because of my *waning years*
and *realization* of their *impracticality:*
At age 79, now, I'm looking at
the eventual termination of my existence
here on Terra Firma––Earth
and what may lie beyond and before me
in another realm where self-shaping
may be a God-forsaken endeavor.

Blessing
(my Forebears)

My interest in genealogy
leads me to wonder:
How far back do my ancestors go?
Reading about ancient history
and human evolution, about the evolution
of life from its very beginnings
guides me to plunder
into this speculation:
Will I meet in Eternity,
in God's heavenly kingdom
all of my forebears
who came before me
——back to the very first amoeba?
My blessing upon them
may they still be inspirited.

Fundamental
(ist)

I am not a fundamentalist
although I was in younger years
but have since seen into the cracks
and crevices of human inventiveness
and don't believe any recorded scripture
was written by God or any angelic
being or supernatural entity:
Human authors have given us scriptures
of many types and stripes and colorings
that we should study and regard reverentially
but not to the point of pounding certainty
that such and only such is always
and always forever absolute in verity:
Wholeness of vision is within human reaching.

Omissions
(sans Commissions)

I have relatives and I have acquaintances
who operatively lack in their makeups
graciousness
for generous acknowledgement
of extended offerings proffered to them
out of affections and fellow camaraderie:
Those omissions serve to signal
missing ingredients in their characters
that would show a warmth
of fellow feelings
for their kindred of relative relatedness
either of blood or community association
that once was paramount
of some companionship interpersonal:
Should such omissiveness be forgiven
or recognized as offensive dullness?

Books
(bought)

I buy a lot of books
and read extensively
but do not read
all the books I buy:
I've looked over every book
that I have bought
and also buy for the library
of my making for the future:
You may very well be
an enlightened reader
of some of my books
that are intended to be housed
in the Founder's Room
of the Genealogy Centers
I hope will be built
in the early 22nd Century.
To you I wish some pleasant
informative reading!

Gross
(ignorance)

Gross ignorance is native to humanity
in individual persons coming up from infancy
and in the infancy of human evolution
and communities and societies of the past:
Gross ignorance is a natural phenomenon
and is innocent in its early beginnings
but warrants correcting as life grows older
and submits to a learning of human progression:
Each individual and every society
bears responsibility for seeking enlightenment
into the origins of myriad developments:
All have a call to upward expansion
of knowledge, appreciation
and unending wonder.

Disappointing
(audience)

When I present to you
a number of suggestions
——thoughts that might provoke you
into responding appropriately
that you then say nothing to
——give no responsive recognition of——
what then am I to surmise
but that you are prudishly dodging
ducking, sidestepping, avoiding
shirking, evading, eluding
skirting, turning from, deflecting
sliding, slipping and parrying from
forthright, wholesome repartee
——what then can I conjecture (?):
That you are a **disappointing audience**
unwilling to be **responsive**
to my frank, sincere
exploratory utterances.
What we have here are **blockages**
to **healthy** communication.

Compassion
(lacking)

One cannot move forward
in the exchange of ideas
when there exists a rampart
of compassion lacking
—a condition of resistance
to illumination and enlightenment
a refusal to listen
to be informed and initiated
into different ways of thinking
of feeling and participating
to the end that maturity
of insight grows steadily
within one's inner center
of kenosis and caring.

Tough-minded (Self-criticism)

Tough-minded self-criticism?
Is this something you've indulged in
in your past or in your present
something taken seriously to heart
pursued with rigor and earnest vigor?
Is this even on your radar
of self-awareness and circumspection
something you've given time to
to rectify your possible faultiness
immaturity and unreflectiveness?
Many will surely not chastise you
for your failure in this arena
for they themselves are uniformly oblivious
to look within to make discoveries.
Is this something you should thus attend to?

Christian
(forgiveness)

Those of you who claim to be Christians,
followers of Christ and his many teachings
show yourselves, ironically, to be most oblivious
to his major teaching of forgiveness and forgiving:
Festering resentments and hostile attributions
reveal your Souls to be grossly ignorant
and maladaptive to Christ's directives
to change your ways and inner Opus!
Such composition of inner malevolence/malefaction
is clearly a signaling of towering crassness,
incivility and personal coarseness
that openly characterizes a Soul's incompleteness,
naïveté and failed self-correctioning:
Are you capacious enough to start
forgiving yourself and Christian amelioration?

Peaks
(and Valleys)

My life experiences have been
a series of peaks and
nearly bottomless valleys
and always at their core and base
have been obscure musical emotions
that have colored those many moments
and propelled my living ever forward:
Between those varied peaks and valleys
there stretched opaque and level plains
to separate and divide
the highs and lows of those experiences:
Isn't this the same for everyone
everyone of human stripe
who enters into this noisome fray
to come and go into eternity?

Musical
(ears)

Some simply don't have
musical ears--they can't hear
the strains and plains
of life and love
that go on around them
always and ever
for the fine tuning-in
that requires little effort:
Growing in stature-sensibility
stipulates some attention
but nothing excessive
in self-exertion:
Some accomplish this
with polymorphous enthusiasm
while others languish
on shores of obliquity.

Reality
(Done to Us?)

We are born into this world
and progress through our infancy
to our childhood years
thence to our adolescence
and young adulthood
then beyond to our maturity
careers and marriage
all the while struggling
with a reality that engages us
never really suspecting
all is being done to us:
Does this seem at all possible?
Does God control our DNA?
Our destinies? Our individual natures?
Is this idea at all appealing
to our individual natures?
Our spirit of freedom?
What about our futures in Eternity?
Is free will an illusion?
Many experiences seem incontrovertible!

Human
(flexibility)

Human flexibility in social relationships
is significant for the perceiving person
who wishes and seeks to blend with others
that agreeable interchanges may transpire.
Persons who present with discordant animus
wreck the peaceful exchanging thus wanted
and make interactions variously distasteful
and spoil camaraderie sorely sought.
Human passionate assertiveness offered
against the grain of congeniality
makes the interchanging rudely dismal
and creates unhappiness corrosively mutual:
Seeking accord is a natural propensity
for all who desire more positive proceedings:
This should not be a difficult doing
for those who desire social stimulating.

CHARACTER, LOVE
and
VISION

Character
(counts)

What should the bottom line be
for one's eternal salvation?
Regardless of what religionists tell us
is of utmost importance––
"following their humanly imposed strictures"
the real bottom line as I fathom it
is the practice of humane *good character*
that even atheists routinely practice
and most non-believers (also good people).
Human decency is human good sense
which is no rubics cube for figuring out:
Who would you want to live with for all eternity:
People of good character
or liars, thieves, rapists and murderers?

Character
(counseling)

There is a need
for character counseling
of every youth
of any age
for educating rightly
sound human behavior
that sends them forth
into their futures
as players in
the social fabric
of life and living
that continues forward
into a lengthy future
that may carry them
to an eternal destiny.

Responsibility
(matters)

What holds things together?
In human relationships
in social interactions
in every facet of lived life
responsibility is the glue
that holds all together:
Everyone knows this
intuitively and existentially.
How often does anyone abide
betrayals, mistreatments
disregards, abuses
all forms of ignoble behavior?
Responsibility is the glue
that holds all together!
Conscientious dependability!

Overall
(development)

Reflect on and consider
your overall development:
What has been uppermost
in your desires and strivings?
Seeking for material gains,
pleasures of the body,
egocentric self-centeredness,
disconnection from others?
There are many ways
one might develop wrongly,
but the better path
is loving kindness,
concern for virtue
and upright actions.

Self
(criticizing)

How profoundly do you do this,
looking at your self self-critically
not to undermine integrity
but to sanitize your honesty
to come full circle with your interior
where your heart and soul cohabit?
Self-criticizing practices
may insure your higher spirit
to those genuine goals and principles
that directives are in scriptures.
Purging false emotions
and wayward inclinations
may make a better person
for your ultimate advent celestial?

Awakening
(the Soul)

What is it one seeks
in libraries, schools and books
that can make a difference
in one's development and goals
if not the enrichment
of one's very own soul?
The richness of character
the nourishment of words
the thoughts and ideas
in the literature observed
makes good for the bolstering
of one's growth of soul
from beginning to end
in life's trajected flow:
It's awakening always
to the new and the bold?

Exceptional
(individuals)

Throughout and before recorded history
there have been exceptional individuals
who have provided leadership and inspiration
to those many others who've surrounded them
or learned about them by word or record:
One grows and develops with an interest
in those individuals exceptional to them
or hopes, oneself, to become one of them
by dint of effort and self-exertion
and always the wonder is whence the origin
of that ascendance falls to those so blessed
to assume their mantle of heroic stature
——is it Fate and Happy Fortuity
or is it something God disposes on them?
Whatever the source of one's true greatness
the work of reality is always before one:
Strive always, therefore, to serve what is noble
and you will surely then enter the Hallways
of what is truly most worthy of Exceptional?

Looking
(Inward)

You don't understand me
--you're projecting animus,
angry resentment, discolorations
that show you're not addressing
yourself in guilty assessment:
Introspection and self-appraisal
are difficult if not impossible
for many (most?) of humanity
but doesn't therefore qualify
for exemption from appraisement
of weak and faulty character
constitution and morality:
Looking down is all too easy,
looking inward shows integrity.

Closed-minded
(and Controlling)

Who do you know or have known
that is closed-minded and controlling
that has limited acceptance
and compassion
for others' views or viewpoints
that may be growing or in transit
to other destinations non-tyrannical?
This/these individual(s) impose limits
on themselves and others
that serve to truncate and to hinder
to impede, constrict and lessen
to repress, suppress and tighten
to modify, qualify and not broaden
others' horizons to greater self-discovery
and expanded self-possession.

Enduring
(North Star)

We cannot indisputably prove
the existence of God
but we can give honor
to our highest yearnings
for what we hold to be true
and of everlasting value:
Reality doesn't offer us
a perfectly clear direction
for placing our hopes and desires
in what is finally bona fide
authentic and genuinely true--
but the composition of character
that resides in each of us
can give us an enduring
North Star.

Exceptional
(quality)

What is "exceptional quality"
in a person of one's acquaintance?
It may be physiognomic beauty
that one is simply born with
or some sparkling intelligence
one acquires with diligent effort
––it may be sterling character
one develops in social transactioning
or it may be a devotion
to an ideal in one's visioning
--it could be a loyalty
one carries in one's heart
it might even be a proneness
to respecting truth
in one's commitment to thinking.

Tests
(of Time)

Who really manages to do this:
To stay the course—
to endure the tests of time?
Who starts with a set of emotions
and keeps them through thick and thin
who doesn't divorce from another
but works to adjust and to alter
to avoid mis-steps or to falter
on the upward path to departure
from life in this world to hereafter?
Enduring the tests of time
may be difficult or easy
but staying the course through time
should yield one a badge of honor?

Question
(of Consciousness)

What is it that engages you?
A myriad of matters––projects––
that occupy your time and attention
some that you build your life upon
––vectors of career and other endeavors
that constitute your very being:
All of this does mightily form
your consciousness––your identity
that makes you entirely who you are.
The question of consciousness
radiates outwardly from you
and fashions the fabric of your goals
it determines the quality of your character
and embellishes the color of your soul.

Open Head
(Open Heart)

Is it really so difficult
to maintain an open head
and a truly open heart,
to keeping pathways open
to newly animated thoughts
and unusual magnificent feelings
that might just transform
one's thinking and emoting
to the end that transfiguration
might arise upright within one
thus changing quite severely
one's landscape (mind and heart)
to realizations of significance
in height and width and depth?
Is this really so difficult
to be scientific in one's reasoning
and resplendent in one's heartstrings?

Simple
(summation)

The Bible is errant
full of misguidance about God
is a human product
full of human proclivities
and a fallible attempt
to articulate what God might be:
Bottom line——human behavior
should strive to be good
——man is imperfect, prone to error
does not one see this
in the Bible itself?
Believe and practice goodness
strive always for wholeness
practice love and compassion
mercy and forgiveness and
do your best to live soundly:
Work at this ardently?

Contentment
(and Meaning)

Recognize this within oneself
and thus with all who have ever lived:
Going home to warmth and security
to embrace the Love
one should happily find there
is ultimate haven for living souls
—the **feeling** of **completeness**
at one's hearth-stone:
All who have lived
must surely know in the soul
the heart of one's feelings
for the grace of this
wholeness of contentment and meaning:
Life should be Love for all of humanity
for one's fellows' feelings all told.
Shouldn't this resonate in each of our souls?

Bottomline
(love)

The upper limit and bottomline
of human relatedness should be
a holding to a standard of love
that stands above other considerations:
What is in one's heart if not such love?
Love of family, love of neighbor,
love of community, nation, planet,
––love of self does point this way
if not distorted by self-aggrandizement.
Complexities of life
can induce short-sidedness,
come to disregard others' quality of life
and this condition, an existential distortion,
alters unhappily what is most desirable:
A bottomline love that holds all together.

Conveying
(sentiments)

Conveying sentiments is all too easy
for those empowered with such aplomb
and graced with similar good-will feelings
that, unfortunately, we can find lacking
in those of many dissimilar dispositions.
Communication is a bed-rock essential
indispensable for promoting understanding
and luxurious comprehensive awareness
of multiple matters bearing on complex reality:
Knowledge is part of human responsibility
unto others as is our sentience
of human feelings and commiseration:
One's gravitas in all things human
submits gracefully to conveying sentiments.

Evolving Away
(from Love)

It takes some time
and a strong conscience
to grow the stamina
to evolve away from love
——a love that is futile
for want of reciprocity
that is not mutual
yet still uncompromised
by the one loving
an inflexible other
who is stuck on some notion
of superior virtue
that knows no compassion
mercy or dispensation.

Enduring
(respectfulness)

Cinders and ashes are surely disheartening
if one should inherit such a damning disaster
but perhaps its antidote is something special
that goes under the byword of something familiar
that occurs naturally from infancy forward
that all experience at least in some measure
and hopefully more frequently than any other
––the happy reality of **finding true love**
that endures well beyond any brief infatuation
or piquant sensation of the internal senses:
The finding of love should be applicable
to an entire universe of deserving others
that oversees and transcends
momentary distresses
to embrace comprehensively
enduring **respectfulness**.

Continuing Love
(and Concern)

How often have you ever experienced
continuing love and concern
from those you've known or favored
for their contributions to your person?
Isn't it natural and spontaneous
to shower others with one's feelings
for their presence, their existence
in one's life-space and one's prevalence?
Isn't it normal to love freely
those who give you responsive feelings
for your persistence in their living
in their existence, day-life being?
Continuing concern and love is reciprocal
for all who've contributed correspondingly.

Reciprocal
(love)

How long can one carry on
without reciprocal love
in a relationship
that doesn't support
intellectual and emotional
nourishment and enrichment?
Yes, one can settle into
a tolerable togetherness
devoid of passion
or meaningful stimulation
but in that case
the heart runs on empty
the mind becomes benumbed
and life experiences impersonal flicker
of mutual acquaintance
and boring entitlements:
Such a life is hardly worth living?

Empathic
(bond)

You're in a relationship
of some depth and substance:
Can you make a measurement
of the empathy between you
toward the other
or that coming to you?
Your future relationship
with that other
will ultimately hinge upon
the empathy coursing between you
the qualities of character
and the adhesive adherence
that operates between you:
Mutual respect and regard
will determine its endurance.

Considered
(forgiveness)

How does one acquire
love and compassion
when reality presents one
many negative experiences
that inspire manifold resentments
to be acted on with intensity
and ravenous displeasure?
Only an indwelling spirit
of considered forgiveness
can help such affliction
to achieve self-transcendence
and a measure of tolerance
for human miscreance
and asininity unspeakable.

Enduring
(Love)

Initial and continuing attraction, acceptance
a commitment to shared higher principles
a wish and desire for a stable relationship
allowance and tolerance for varying behaviors
a refusal to indulge in promiscuous temptations
knowledge that life is subject to vicissitudes
acquiescence to changing circumstances
a willingness and need to keep things together
some talent for creating a lively variety
in the everyday interactions of two individuals
character stability in pursuance of careers
a dependable reliance in fiscal management
honorable goals two can agreeably pledge to:
These are some of the essentials mandatory
to ensuring an enduring love.

Penetrating
(introspection)

What is in your heart? Do you really know?
How soundly are you in touch
with your deepest longings and feelings?
Are you capable of correcting
your erroneous thoughts and impulses?
Have you ever recognized faults within yourself
and confessed them to your higher Self, to God?
How important is it to you
to be totally honest with yourself and others?
Have you often or ever conducted
a penetrating introspection of your soul?
These are questions I have asked myself:
Are they merely questions I've asked of myself
or do they warrant a broader application
to all who seek to plumb the truths
of human reality, our universal existence?
Are you inclined to regard these questions **reductively**
to assign them to the margins of your awareness?
How important is it to be **honest** with yourself
and thus with others of your acquaintance?
Are these questions tendencious and laborious?
Is there anyone you would share your answers with?
Or is this asking far too much for you to converse with
——even of yourself? ? ? ? ? ? ?

Thinking
(outside the box)

How sorely difficult is it
to think outside the box
of your mental configurations
you have built on sour emotions?
What heart-felt feelings are missing
in your attitudes and assumptions
that give guidance to your stances
that obliterate compassionate caring?
Hardness of heart is **blinding**
to opportunities and perceptions
that give office to redemption,
to forgiveness and to raising
the love you have been given
from those others' graces founding.

Defensive (Rationalizations)

Are you able even remotely
to see yourself in rationalizing
your way forward sans restrictions
on your presumptive considerations?
Have you ever taken moment
to reflect your action-values
that are composed of defensive animus
toward positions counter your anterior?
Defensive rationalizations
are the opposite of sound thinking
that engages head and heart
and loving compassionate caring.
What have you done to reconnoiter
your obstinate mental maneuverings?

Dismissing
(fixations)

Something always difficult to do
but something necessarily imperative
and most especially psychologically
which is to say mentally-emotionally
is the task of **dismissing fixations**
that have formed out of experiences
most especially love experiences
that reveal to be one-sided
that were never truly reciprocal
unrequited, unreturned——unhappily:
Why should this be so imperative?
Restoring balance is always the answer
to keep one healthy mentally-emotionally
and out of harm from depressive scenarios.

Extended
(vision)

What on Earth is extended vision?
I think we know we live on Earth,
that our basic existence is grounded here
and even those who venture beyond
intend to return to this home they love.
But what of vision and how extended?
What do we see with myopic eyes?
Do we not need to escape our restive cloisters
to bound beyond our existential confinements?
Mental and emotional conundrums absorb us;
we need to catapult out of our boxes
and begin to view things as *other* terrestrials
start seeing our personal self-imposed internments
and spring outward to extended visions
where greater truths become
characteristic genius.

Higher
(honesty)

Should one marvel at another's
taking offense at one's honesty
when that honesty is offered sincerely
with verifiable, unimpeachable integrity?
Taking offense at one's honesty
raises questions of such revulsion
and implies uneasiness, even anxiety,
with hitherto undeclared truths
in the dialogue of correspondence:
Such anxiety brokers hyper-sensitivity
to matters wished to remain unspoken
––even hidden––in that dialogue
that wishes to move to greater openness
and transparency, yes, and thence
to **higher honesty.**

Unconquered
(spirit)

What is it that resides
in one's human person
that strives to endure
against all opposing odds
over periods of time
in various environs
if not the will, the need and desire
to persevere and reign triumphant
over every antithesis encountered
in the drama of lived life?
The heart and soul of that tenacity
its vigor of highest yearning
must finally be crowned
one's all absorbing
unconquered spirit.

Emotional
(life)

Where do we live but in
our emotional life of sensibility?
We live grounded in emotions
that underlie all our living
that have united with our attachments
to the many specifics of our environment:
People, places and things,
our ideas of reverence
constitute our living space
of allegiances and pledges.
That life can be transcended
by exercise of one's Reason
and can give newer fidelity
to constructs of contemplation.

Constructs
(of Contemplation)

Constructs of contemplation
must square with living reality
if they are to be counted
as legitimate benchmarks
for living a life of prominence:
Why then prominence?
Prominence is living
to a standard of personal integrity
that incorporates sound strivings
for excellence in living.
Excellence, then, may be measured
by what is naturally possible
for one's individual potential
in the matrix of one's
Worldly Vision.

Newer
(vision)

Each appears and grows to adulthood
and takes on exposure to influences about
and then assumes a specific identity
about oneself, the world and reality without:
What one assumes of important questions
and decides what is accurate, what not,
is a function of a matrix of experiences:
What one aspires to is part of that matrix
and makes for those interests one's life is about
but who dares to question his verities and certainties
becomes a pioneer into the forest of doubt
where convictions break down and flounder about
until newer vision makes for peace and redoubt.
This is accomplished through earnest effort?

Postscript

Speaking truth
(to power)

Speaking truth to power
may not make things right
but will provide some solace
to the inevitable fight
one wages in the light
of contradictory claims
that occur when divisions spike:
Love is always most right
when clashes occur
whatever the outcome
when oppositions pledge plight
for honor, duty and truth
in the light and the fight
for humanity and for goodness
over blight.

Uncomfortable
(questions)

Asking uncomfortable questions
is the work of intelligence:
If one is to learn uniformly
about one's surrounding reality
it becomes imperative to probe
unreservedly into operative actions
that impinge upon that which
confronts one.
Only by asking such questions
that may discomfort others
—or even oneself—
can **truth** be apprehended
and reality laid bare:
Suppression and repression
prove to be costly investments.

Questionably
(God given?)

We are products of our inheritance
genetic codes that naturally control us
--each has his/her own dna makeup
from which there is no jumping out of:
We can look around and see our betters
and know they have superior makeups
that do propel them to greater heights
to which we others may aspire
but cannot touch on final account of
many factors that do naturally control us:
Ultimately we need to reconcile self
with limitations that do prevent us
from climbing those heights
that do inspire us... .
Thus our natures are questionably God given.?

Everlasting
(Eternity)

Why should reality change
in an everlasting eternity?
The scope of your life
is mixed––good and bad
with highs and lows
and in-betweens:
Whence comes the notion
that the afterlife would be different?
Why should God manifest differently
than He has throughout history?
Have our thinkers and scribblers
imagined so narrowly
that our reality in Eternity
should somehow be transcendent?
'Heavenly bliss' may be false imagining.

Eventual
(demise)

How am I feeling
about my eventual demise?
I'm not feeling sorry for myself
——all of my ancestors
have passed that way.
One doesn't think about dying
in one's youth——for me long passed
--now that I'm older
easily past eight decades
and acceptabley a mature adult
I recognize the inevitable
from which there is no escape:
Others' may practice avoidance;
acquiescene is the practical scape.

Essence
(supersedes Existence)

What, then, is the business of existence
if not to seek and to pursue
to follow a calling of one's spirit
to reach for higher things
for that that is more essential
to one's living and one's treasured existence?
What are such treasured things?
Do not all have a sense of something larger
something more than of passing importance
something that looms larger than one's Self?
Could that something larger be a sense of God
a Being who creates and encompasses the world
a Being one might call the Ground of Being
who is the creator and provider of Life
who gives us direction for our ultimate Essence?

*These lyrics are better listened to than read.
This is the third stanza of Stevens' lyrics
with the essential message that
"everybody is a radio receiver" so
"turn your radio on ...get in touch with God."

**Ray Stevens' Lyrics:
Turn your Radio On**

A don't you know that **everybody is a radio receiver**
All you gotta do is listen for the call
Turn your radio on - turn your radio
Turn your radio on - turn your radio on
If you listen in you will be a believer
Leanin' on the truth that will never fail
Get in touch with God - get in touch with God
Turn your radio on

$\mathfrak{Some}$ of my "$\mathfrak{Musical}$ $\mathfrak{Ears}$"

Musical Journey

<u>Innocence/Wonderment</u>

Born Free ....Roger Williams
What A Wonderful World ....Louis Armstrong
Games People Play ....Joe South
Greenback Dollar...........................Kingston Trio
Stranger On The Shore .... Acker Bilk

<u>Dreaming</u>

Dream A Little Dream Of Me............. Mama Cass
Mary In There Morning......................... Al Martino
Calcutta ....Lawrence Welk Orchestra
Beyond The Sea...............................Bobby Darin
The Impossible Dream.......................Jack Jones

<u>Adventuring</u>

A Swinging Safari .... Billy Vaughn
Anything Goes ....Harpers Bizarre
Mame ....Louis Armstrong
Gentle On My Mind....................... Glen Campbell
I Remember You .... Frank Ifeld

<u>Loving</u>

When I Fall In Love .... The Lettermen
The Way You Look Tonight............ The Lettermen
Tonight.....................................Ferrante & Teicher
Whispering ....Nino Tempo & April Stevens
Since I Fell For You........................... Lenny Welch

<u>Breaking Up</u>

A Man Without Love........................ The Lettermen
Break It To Me Gently.......................... Brenda Lee
A Little Bitty Tear......................................Burl Ives
Cara Mia............................ Jay & The Americans
Hurt So Bad.................................. The Lettermen

<u>Reckoning</u>

Try A Little Kindness...................... Glen Campbell
Put A Little Love
    In Your Heart ....Brenda Lee
Here In My Heart ....Al Martino
My Cup Runneth Over ....Ed Ames
Kiss Me Goodbye ....Petula Clark

FOLLOW THE BEAT

Buckaroo .... Buck Owens
Are You Ready For The Country .... Waylon Jennings
The Story Of Your Life Is In Your Face........................... Tom T. Hall
Open Up Your Heart.. Buck Owens
You Don't Know Me ....Ray Charles
I'm Gonna' Write A Song .... Tommy Cash
Country Is ....Tom T. Hall
Rose Garden .... Lynn Anderson
Misty .... Ray Stevens
Just Between You And Me ....Charley Pride
Billy Ray Wrote A Song .... George Jones
A Few Old Country Boys ....Randy Travis & George Jones
Life's Little Ups And Downs .... Charlie Rich
I Love You Because... Jerry Lee Lewis
Love's Gonna' Live Here .... Buck Owens
For The Heart...Elvis Presley
Me And Bobby McGee .... Jerry Lee Lewis
A Week In A Country Jail ....Tom T. Hall
Unwind .... Ray Stevens
Love Me...Elvis Presley
My Heart Cracked But It Did Not Break.......................Randy Travis
There's A Little Bit Of Hank In Me ....Charley Pride
Take Me Home Country Roads .... John Denver
A Hundred Years From Now..Elvis Presley
I'll Go To My Grave Loving You .... The Statler Brothers
You've Still Got A Place In My Heart..................... Jerry Lee Lewis
The Ride .... David Alan Coe
Could I Have This Dance?.. Anne Murray

Musical Story Lines

The "In" Crowd .... The Ramsey Lewis Trio
Missin' You ....Charley Pride
I Care...Tom T. Hall
To A Sleeping Beauty..Jimmy Dean
Spiders And Snakes... Jim Stafford
A Real Good Time... Jim Stafford
Hello Josephine.. Jerry Lee Lewis
Your Molecular Structure.. Mose Allison
T-R-O-U-B-L-E .... Travis Tritt
Margie .... Jerry Lee Lewis
The Old School... John Conlee
Old Friends.. Roger Miller w/Ray Price
Hope You're Feelin' Me Like I'm Feelin' You ....Charley Pride
Someone Loves You Honey ....Charley Pride

+++++++++++++++++++++++++++++++++

Why You Been Gone So Long..................................... Tommy Cash
You Don't Hear .... Tommy Cash
My Girl Bill .... Jim Stafford
Hit The Road Jack..Ray Charles
Kentucky Rain .... Elvis Presley
A Little Bitty Tear ....Burl Ives
Born To Lose .... Jerry Lee Lewis
Hello Walls...Willie Nelson
Walkin' The Floor Over You................................... Jerry Lee Lewis
Honey ....Bobby Goldsboro
He Stopped Loving Her Today ....George Jones
If I'm A Fool For Loving You .... Elvis Presley
Why Don't You Love Me...Charley Pride
Let Me Live In The Light Of His Love ....Charley Pride

THE BEAT GOES ON

Song & Melodies

Some Favorite Films

This listing leaves out numerous other categories including:
Action; Americana––Early; Animals; Biography; Boxing; Civil
War; Crime; Drama; Fantasy; Horror; Mystery––Suspense––
Thrillers; Noir; Political; Prisoners––Escapes––Isolated––
Marginalized; Religious; Sci-Fi; Spirituals; Sports; and War.

Supreme Favorites

Spartacus	El Cid	Braveheart
Troy	The Fall of the Roman Empire	300
Julius Caesar	Cleopatra	Gladiator
Alexander	Alfred the Great	War Lord
Henry V	Becket	Rob Roy
First Knight	Waterloo	Patton

Adventure

The Vikings	The Adventures of Robin Hood	Ben Hur
The Three Musketeers	Gone With the Wind	The Count of Monte Cristo
Moby Dick	Robin Hood: Prince of Thieves	Captain Blood
Tom Jones	The Man Who Would Be King	The Mask of Zorro
Barry Lyndon	The Lion In Winter	Doctor Zhivago

Comedies

Airplane!	Dr. Strangelove	Young Frankenstein
Office Space	Dirty Rotten Scoundrels	Groundhog Day
The Jerk	Robin Hood: Men in Tights	The Naked Gun
Hot Shots	Hot Shots: Part Deux	Three Amigos
Roxanne	Play It Again, Sam	One Fine Day

Courtroom Dramas

Jagged Edge	12 Angry Men	Class Action
A Few Good Men	Witness for the Prosecution	To Kill a Mockingbird
Primal Fear	Anatomy of a Murder	Inherit the Wind
The Accused	Judgment at Nuremberg	Philadelphia

Musicals

The Music Man	Yankee Doodle Dandy	Oklahoma!
My Fair Lady	West Side Story	Porgy and Bess
Camelot	Singin' in the Rain	Show Boat
Chicago	Meet Me In St. Louis	Easter Parade
Carousel	In the Good Old Summertime	Viva Las Vegas

Romance

Wuthering Heights	Random Harvest	Waterloo Bridge
Picnic	Far From the Madding Crowd	Love Story
Revenge	Love Is A Many-Splendored Thing	Titanic
Serendipity	An Officer and A Gentleman	Pretty Woman
Ghost	The Fabulous Baker Boys	The Way We Were
Roxanne	Jerry Maguire	Always

Westerns

One-Eyed Jacks	Once Upon A Time In the West	The Appaloosa
The Last Sunset	Last Train From Gun Hill	Lonely Are the Brave
High Noon.	Ride the High Country	Shane
The Long Riders	The Wild Bunch	Red River
Wyatt Earp	The Magnificent Seven	Tombstone
3;10 to Yuma	Butch Cassidy and the Sundance Kid	Unforgiven
Viva Zapata	The Outlaw Josey Wales	The Gunfighter
Dances With Wolves	Duel In the Sun	The Searchers
Open Range	Bite the Bullet	Silverado
A Man Called Horse	Man In the Wilderness	The Missing
The Missouri Breaks	Jeremiah Johnson	Dodge City
The Jack Bull	Gunfight at the O. K. Corral	The Big Sky
Nevada Smith	They Died With Their Boots On	Jesse James
Hombre	The Big Country	Maverick

Other Favorites

Plymouth Adventure	The Last of the Mohicans	The Patriot
Hidalgo	The Black Stallion	Secretariat
Casino Royale	Predator	Taken
Amadeus	The Private Lives of Elizabeth and Essex	Lust for Life
Hard Times	Cinderella Man	The Greatest
Lincoln	Ken Burns' The Civil War	Gettysburg
No Way Out	Crime and Punishment	Payback
The Fountainhead	The Light Between Oceans	The Caine Mutiny
House of Games	Who's Afraid of Virginia Wolf?	On the Waterfront
Excalibur	What Dreams May Come	Meet Joe Black
The Exorcist	The Thing From Another World	Jaws
The Andromeda Strain	2001: A Space Odyssey	A Clockwork Orange
Double Indemnity	The Godfather Trilogy	The Sting
The Shawshank Redemption	The Bridge On the River Kwai	Robinson Crusoe
Les Miserables	A Tale of Two Cities	The Razor's Edge
Last Year at Marienbad	The Manchurian Candidate	Woman in the Dunes
The Ten Commandments	The Passion of the Christ	Joan of Arc

Educating
(Mind and Heart)

Books seek to educate one's mind
enlarging its essential awareness
introducing subjects new
expanding those in great detail
giving expanse to ever new vistas
presenting challenges
to one's thinking
causing thoughts to come alive.
Movies move to educate the heart
producing depths within and out
enlarging one's emotional marrow
presenting relationships
right and wrong
inspiring social/psychological
realities to adopt/eschew
firming strong one's inner fiber.

ADDENDA

Richmond Pass

She was sitting in the bleachers with her two best friends. The day had been filled with excitement. It was Homecoming Day! She had risen early to join her classmates in a labor of love. They were adding finishing touches to the Junior class float for the afternoon parade. She had volunteered to serve as co-chairman of the float's decoration committee, and was filled with the sheer joy of being involved.

On the second play following the opening kickoff a Spartan halfback ran 72 yards up the middle for a touchdown. Only one minute into the game, and the Bluejays were already six points behind. Sandra felt a fearful piercing and the day's joy escape like cold air from a rubber balloon. In a somewhat similar way she had endured the reality of another loss when the judges had given first prize to the Sophomore float. But she had not been alone when that took place. Chance had been with her and had comforted her plentifully.

"I'm not talking while the flavor lasts" he beamed jokingly as he hugged her generously and sank his face into lustrous brown hair while kissing her neck below the right ear. His pun was directed at the float's name which had been Sandra's noodle. She had thought it up herself after dozens of suggestions had been considered and rejected. She knew how much the hometown, the school, the team, and especially Chance had wanted a victory for this occasion. His unmitigated drive for success on the playing field she sensed as a raging, ravenous appetite in him. And that's where she got the idea for a Liberty Bluejay chewing on the arm of a Richmond Spartan. The two figures were shown on a simulated football field. The idea was typical, a reflection of her hearty imagination. She had remarkable ability to express such thoughts with a charming, unselfconscious frankness. It was one of her strongest traits and, aside from her beauty, the feature Chance Hartman enjoyed most in her.

It had been a beautiful Autumn day. October in Missouri was always special, a reminder of the change of season within the spirit as without. The early morning air had a crispness about it that felt really good. Only a few clouds had hung in the morning sky, giving the sun a small obstacle course from which to burst continually forth. The red-yellow-brown of leaves and trees possessed a freshness Sandra loved with unreflected yearning. Her beauty formed a perfect match to nature's: Patrician nose, occasional freckles on smooth, clear skin, medium brown hair, distinctively curved lips and hazel eyes set to an innocent, wholesome face could have caused an angel to sing in praise. She was a lovely youth.

The Bluejays fought back, moved the ball 65 yards down the field before being held off at the 11 yard line. The first quarter ended with Richmond ahead, 6 - 0. Sandra reflected back on the afternoon's events. Chance had left her side to mount the Courthouse steps where he joined the team's other two co-captains. The Homecoming Queen and her two attendants were to be announced. Sandra herself held no expectations, but it had grieved Chance that his sweetheart had not received recognition. The Queen and her two attendants were nominated and elected exclusively by the team's 36 members. Sandra had not been elected. The whole thing had been political, with players voting in cliques. It was a fragmented affair. The Queen herself had achieved the august crown by a slender margin and the total approval of six votes. Michele Parrish was dutifully crowned. Chance felt no elation that she had been his seventh-grade sweetheart. He himself had crowned the first attendant, Peggy Taylor. He was glad when the business was ended. He wanted to get back to Sandra McQuarrie.

In the second quarter the Spartans rushed within 10 yards of scoring on two separate series. The Bluejays held them valiantly, but were unable themselves to move the ball effectively. With two minutes to go before the half, another Spartan halfback romped for 32 yards around left end and a second score. This time the try for extra point was good. The first half ended, score Richmond 13 - Liberty 0.

Chance returned to Sandra, shook hands with several well-wishers toward the evening's upcoming contest, and together they departed from the crowd. He drove them to his grandmother's house where his parents and younger brother would return. They had driven in from out of state for a week's visit in the hometown, and had brought Chance's automobile with them.

"The old Olds still runs pretty well" he reflected. He was glad to have it back.

Chance's parents had moved away at the end of his Sophomore year. He had left Liberty reluctantly, and had not adjusted well to the city he'd been brought. That summer had been pretty dismal, but a phone call from the Liberty High football coach had changed all that. The coach had offered, gratis the Junior Chamber of Commerce, to send him plane fare if he would come back to play ball. It was his earnest desire to finish his high school days in his old hometown. His parents finally relented and allowed his wish. Now, in his Senior year, he would have the further privilege of access to a car—his car. He loved his hometown, he loved his family and friends and Nature. In sum, he loved. It was a mighty thing and all unconscious, except for how he felt for Sandra. That was a burning, longing love, somewhat like his love for sports. He felt the glimmerings of exaltation when he was with her and even more so when he wasn't. Now, in the latening afternoon, he would have to take her home and prepare for the evening's game.

As they drove toward the downtown square, rays of sunlight scattered off of autumn trees as the sun began to sink in the western sky. Both felt the numinous glow of reflected energy flowing fro and from their youthful bodies. The were a happy, compatible pair.

"I remember feeling how ferocious you seemed in grade school" Sandra Said.

"Yeah, I guess I was a bully" Chance offered back. "But I never beat on little girls" he mockingly replied.

They both laughed. The beauty and energy of their youth were beyond their powers to articulate. The just knew it felt very good to be in each other's company.

After pulling up in front of Sandra's house, he cut the ignition and set the brake. Then he turned to embrace her in his arms. They melted together as in a dream. Passionately, they kissed.

"Well, I better go" Chance spoke at last.

"Then you'll pick me up here after the game?" she asked.

"Yeah. It'll probably be 10:30 or so. I sure hope we win. It won't be much of a dance if we don't."

"Keep your spirits high" Sandra cheered.

They walked to the door and embraced again. He turned, then, and set his mind on the game ahead.

At the halftime ceremonies, the Liberty High band performed several numbers and then presented a skit showing the Bluejays running away with the game. Nearly everyone wondered at that. The halftime score certainly suggested otherwise. The floats were driven around the track outlying the field, and the Homecoming Queen and her attendants were again presented to the admiring crowd. A spirit of jubilation and unhappy despondency hung in the air. And then the Bluejays charged back onto the field.

Sandra crossed her fingers and stood for the opening kickoff. Bobby Lawrence, the Bluejay quarterback, caught it on the 10 yard line and carried it to the 30. A quick succession of short runs and flat-zone passes brought them to the opponents 19. But there they stalled and lost their fourth down bid for eight inches and a first-and-ten. The turnover was fortuitous. Richmond ran two plays for twelve and fifteen yards each. And then a flat-zone pass to their left end was intercepted by Larry Criswell. He scooted 49 yards and hit pay dirt for a Liberty score. Things were looking up. Chad Hurst's kick made good the extra point. The score was Richmond 13 – Liberty 7.

Sandra and her friends were ecstatic. At last the mood had changed. The Bluejays were beginning to roll. Or so it seemed. The remainder of the third quarter was a tug of war. Neither team could penetrate effectively into the other's territory. It became a defensive battle. Precious yardage would be gained and lost. Both teams punted repeatedly to the other after three to seven downs of play. The spectators began to grow restless. The homeside bleacher crowd could be heard from the field as it yelled and cheered, and then grow silent with the monotony of short yardage gains. The third quarter ended with the score unchanged: Richmond 13 – Liberty 7. In the fourth quarter, Chance broke away from two tacklers for a 22 yard romp down the right side of the field. From his position at left halfback he had looped around to the right and rushed over the right offensive tackle's slot. He had been hit from his left, but had slipped free into the secondary. An outside defensive linebacker had hit him from his right on the downfield break, and had slowed his progress momentarily. A Spartan defensive back had finally brought him down on their sweep to the sideline. The play had brought the crowd to a roar, but an offensive penalty nullified the forward progress. Another play later and the Bluejays were again forced to punt.

The Spartan safety who caught the punt returned the ball to the Liberty 34. The crowd had gone into an uproar over a clipping penalty the Refs had failed to call. The clipping was clearly visible, later, in the game film. The run was good for 52 yards, and the Richmond team was threatening again. On two plays they gained seven yards. On third down a straight hand off to their fullback over the left guard was stopped cold. It was then fourth and three on the Liberty 27. The stadium held its breath. The Spartans came out of the huddle. The Bluejay defense was waiting on the line.

"Watch for the end run" Chance yelled across the field to the right side corner linebacker.

"Plug the line" the defensive safety screamed.

The Spartans lined up.

"Ready, set" their quarterback barked.

"Hut one, hut two, hut three" he yelled.

Chance could see them coming. It was an end run to their right, and they were coming at him. The Spartan offensive end attempted to block him, but Chance was too driven to let it happen. He shoved the would-be blocker aside to his right, and tread the ground beneath him as he layed for the onrushing halfback. The back faked to cut wide outside, but saw immediately he would have to charge head on. The two collided at chest level. Chance hit him high to avoid the risk of no defensive backup behind him. For a moment the two were locked in an embrace, but then went down as Chance wrestled his opponent to the ground. The Spartan threat was temporarily stopped.

From up above, high in the bleachers, Sandra took a deep breath and sighed relief. She was not alone in that. The entire hometown crowd had felt the same.

"Saved again" she thought.

Liberty took over on their own 28. In quick succession they moved the ball to their 50. Time was short and the team knew they had their work cut out. Chance wondered when they were going to throw the pass. They had named it the 'Richmond Pass' precisely for this opponent. They had practiced it methodically for weeks. Just as he was growing restive with the coach's apparent reluctance to use the play, a substitute guard came on the field. He passed the word to Bobby Lawrence, the team quarterback.

There was silence in the huddle. Bobby spoke carefully. "Okay guys, this is the big one. Everybody knows what to do––right? Richmond Pass on three."

They broke the huddle and jogged to the scrimmage line. Chance felt butterflies in his stomach, and wondered if his apprehension was visible on his face. The team lined up.

"Ready, set" Bobby Lawrence yelled out.

The Bluejays hit the three point stance. The count began.

"Hut one, hut two, hut three"

The ball was snapped. Chance charged forward over the left tackle slot immediately ahead. Bobby Lawrence faked a handoff to the fullback charging over the right side center slot, and then dropped back. Both offensive ends made fake blocks, then rushed down field for 12 yards before cutting oppositely to their outsides. The 5-4-2 Richmond defense was completely gulled. Their defensive backs went outside wide to cover the outrushing ends. The downfield center was left wide open.

Bobby Lawrence drifted back from the line of scrimmage. And drifted. He was a master at concealing the ball. Even in the film, later, it was difficult to see he had it.

Chance Hartman raced down field. He was all alone. Time seemed to slow, if not completely stop. He was aware that he was running. Running for the team, running for Sandra, running for the coach, his folks, the crowd, running for glory. He had even spoken to the high school assembly the night before at the pep rally, before they burned the Spartan effigy, the words of Bear Bryant.

"Winning," he said, "isn't everything. It's the only thing!" He believed it, and wanted others to believe it, too. The school crowd and the team. Especially the team. The words were sacred to him.

He was in the open and all alone. He could see the defensive backs were far away. As he continued to run he looked back over his right shoulder. Bobby Lawrence had thrown the ball. It was sailing high into the air, tracing an arc between the 40 yard line and its destination point he knew not where. Chance knew that Bobby had overthrown. He saw with anguish he could not catch it, that it would be impossible to reach. He also knew he had to try.

With resolution that comes from unknown depths, Chance Hartman turned his eyes and head toward his goal. He strained and stretched his body and his arms in a forward running reaching out. He could not now even see the ball. He only knew he had to try. He ran––forward, arms outstretched. If his arms had elevated upward instead of forward, he would have been a spectacle of prayer.

Time. The eternal now. The infinite passing through the finite world. A switch of place to uncanny grace. The overreaching throw of God to man, in a whirl of unrestrained restraint. The darkened sky lit up by brilliant lights. A crowd of hundreds. Eyes all riveted on the eternal finite. A moment of time, in time, out of time, before and after time. The immediate time. The now time.

Chance caught the ball. He never knew how, never understood how it could have happened. All he knew was that his arms reached out, the ball was overthrown, would be impossible to catch. But there it was! In his hands! The ball had landed in his hands!

"Holy god! How could that be?" he wondered.

But he knew what he had to do. As he stumbled forward from his overextended reach, a defensive safety raced upon him. From the 20 yard line where Chance had caught the 'Richmond Pass', he stumbled and fought his way to the five yard line where he was finally brought down.

The moment had been exhilarating and exasperating all at once. It was a coordinated catch. Later in the week, a teammate's uncle's remark would reach his ears.

"Chance sure gave it the 'ol college try on that one!"

The crowd went wild. Chance could hear their roar in his ears. He heard it, then, but immediately ignored. His team had not yet scored.

Sandra beamed in ecstasy at the Chance catch. His parents and little brother weren't unhappy either. A surge of proud and joyous might filled the crowd on that particular night.

Back on the field, two consecutive dive plays had brought the Bluejays to the one yard line. On third down, Bobby looked at Chance with an expression that said, "Okay, pal, this one's for six." On the snap of the ball, Bobby handed it off to Chance. Chance charged the line and leaped into the air. When he came down, he was over the line. The score was tied: Richmond 13 – Liberty 13.

Chad Hurst ran on to kick the extra point. His try was good, and the Bluejays were up on top!

The final two minutes of play were conclusive. The Bluejays were so fired up they forced a fumble at the Richmond 45. And from there they stalled the ball till the clock ran out.

Later, when he picked up Sandra before heading for the dance, her mother gave him an unexpected surprise. It was a small, colorfully wrapped book. When he opened it, he was curiously puzzled. The book was entitled "The Collected Poems of Stephen Crane". Little could he know, then, how profoundly those poems would influence him over the long years ahead.

****

Author's note: The essential core of this story is factual—–the interception, the tackle, the butterflies, the pass, its reception. Liberty won the game by a score of 20 to 6. I scored two touchdowns. The real characters of this story were as follows:

Chance Hartman .... Gentry Thomason
Sandra McQuarrie .... Courtney Roberts
Larry Criswell .... Larry Crisler
Bobby Lawrence .... Larry Driggers
Chad Hurst .... Jim Hurt
Michele Parrish.. Janet Harris
Peggy Taylor.. Joyce Ballew
The Coach .... Phil Miller

The quote that I had researched and attributed to Bear Bryant of Alabama fame I had subsequently learned was originally that of Vince Lombardi.

Author's Photos

More about 10/'64: Travelin'

To round out the story of my auto accident in October of
1964 I need to add the following: The Highway patrolman
who came upon my accident, who investigated that
mishap thoroughly, told me that an elderly gentleman
driving an antique car had passed my rolling Corvair,
by a mere few feet as I rumbled behind him, and would
have killed us both if I had collided with his vehicle.

Aside from my possible death in the accident itself,
a collision would have produced another death
beside my own.

Additionally, I was fortunate that a photographer,
who was employed with The Kansas City Star newspaper,
happened to travel by the scene of my accident and
stopped to volunteer taking photos (eight) of the
start and completion of that event.

I was driving without my seat belt strapped on and was
thrown to the backseat of the Corvair where a metal rod
was anchored above the backseat with my numerous
clothes (shirts, pants, jackets, etc.) hanging.
Those clothes cushioned me as the vehicle rolled and
bounced about. This was another uncanny circumstance
that prevented my head from smashing onto the concrete
road as my car smashed itself onto the opposing lanes.

In all of that accident I was multiply blessed to have
come out with a scratch on the back of my right calf
(through the jeans I was wearing) and small shards
of window glass in my hair.

I could have failed too live this long to become
the author of this book. What an amazing
moment that was in my life.

CAR CRASH

225

Collective Photo

FURTHER THOUGHTS

and

CLARIFICATIONS

Description and Summary

Existential Ruminations is a small encyclopedia of my thoughts (ruminations) on existence and eternity, truth and reality, God, religion and the supernatural, self and others, and character, love and vision. The compelling core of this book has to do with an experience I had in San Diego, California in August of 1979. I had been an atheist for some 20 years, had experienced three psychiatric hospitalizations during the decade of the '70s, and believed I was experiencing demonic affliction. I decided on speaking to a Catholic priest-making confession-for the years of my apostasy. I made that confession in the Priest's office, sitting across from him at his desk. He gave me absolution, and I left to return home. From Regents Road I drove to Clairemont Mesa Boulevard, then turned right on Genesse Avenue heading south. It was getting dark. I turned my headlights on and went into a dip in the road that was covered in fog. I followed the broken white lines to stay in my lane. I knew at the top of that road where it leveled off there was a Christian Church with a large cross atop its building. I wasn't thinking about that at the time, was looking around to get my bearings on exactly where I was. Within seconds I was immediately thunderstruck with the realization I was not where I was supposed to be! I was four miles north and moving in that direction-a slight distance from Scripps Memorial Hospital. I was dumbfounded! It took me short time to realize I had experienced a miracle. On reflection later I surmised that that experience did not follow natural law, that God had interposed to make a statement: That God was real and I was 20 years in the wrong-along with all those others I had accepted as mentors to my unbelief. My reading in the "forest of doubt" from the ages of 19 to 39 is still reflected in my ruminations. I am now a "believer" but still shrouded with questions and misgivings: Puzzled. That puzzlement is apparent in <u>Existential Ruminations</u>. There is no escape from thinking.

Instantaneous
(relocation)

What I experienced in August 1979
was not a flying through the air
and not a beaming up or across
the landscape of Genesee Avenue
in San Diego, California:
It was an **instantaneous relocation**
of my car with me in it––driving
initially south but then discovering
I was heading north four miles away!
How, on earth, does that even happen?
Did I experience some neurological anomaly
plus a time gap I was oblivious to?
Decidedly No! It was **continuous!**
And who but God could manage that?
Do we need to divest
our scientific smugness
and humbly acknowledge
we are God's subjects?
Only God, it seems to me,
could make such manifest!

Philosophical
(implications)

The philosophical implications
of my experience on Genesse Avenue
in San Diego of August 1979
are the following:
There is a power beyond this world
that far exceeds
what is humanly capable
of anything approaching it ...
It is able to surpass —transcend—
the accomplishments of any science
It doesn't find it necessary
to speak any words
expresses itself through actions
what it seeks to imply
decidedly leaves no doubt
of its overarching sublimity:
This, I believe, is what we mean
when we say the word: God.

Richmond Pass

At age 17 a Senior in High School
in Liberty, Missouri, my beloved hometown,
I was a Co-Captain on the football team:
It was Homecoming Day, all exciting!
I had spoken to our classes in assembly
these words--quoting Coach Vince Lombardi:
"Winning isn't everything, it's the only thing!"
On the football field that evening
I caught a pass-play labeled "Richmond Pass"
that was phenomenal and personal to me:
I couldn't see that ball but did reach forward
--was certain it was overthrown:
It landed in my hands: I was astounded!
and remarked in my story the following:
"Holy God, how could that be?!
That was the first of three astounding
striking phenomenal occurrences
I have experienced
I've attributed to the interpositioning
of Divinity.

Striking Phenomenal Parallelisms

Although my story, "Richmond Pass," occurs near the conclusion of my book Existential Ruminations, it was the first of three events in my life that articulate a unique, uncanny and **unexpected** triad forming a triple parallelism. None of my reviewers to date have picked up on this.

The second experience was my auto crash on the Kansas Turnpike (Highway 35) while traveling to San Diego and my parents' residence. Miraculously, I experienced no significant injury during my triple spinning turnovers before landing upright facing the opposite of my original direction. My vehicle suffered a total demolition. I climbed out with a scratch on my right calf and shattered glass in my hair. I was driving without my seatbelt strapped on, and was thrown toward the back seat where I was cushioned by clothing hanging from a horizontal bar.

My third experience was my instantaneous relocation discussed and described in the Introduction to Existential Ruminations.

Consider the number three: What might this number suggest to the observant reader? Consider also my attribution of my instantaneous relocation experience on Genesse Avenue in San Diego in August of 1979: That it could not be explained on scientific grounds, that I attributed it to the workings of Divinity--God, the Holy Spirit--and that I claimed the experience a miracle.

Another occurrence of the number three: My three psychiatric hospitalizations. What should one make of those occurrences? My attribution to the Holy Spirit? The relevance of the Christian Trinity--Father, Son, and Holy Spirit?

For me it is evident (and evidence) of God's interposition into my human, earthly experiencing. Of course, skeptics will oppose this inference, and I can do nothing about that than to draw attention to the parallelisms. I was a twenty years skeptic and atheist myself--but cannot in all honesty and sincerity (authenticity) deny my experiences and what they eloquently and intelligibly say to me.

Historically, traditionally, since the time of the Enlightenment, philosophers have queried about the apparent **masking** of Divine creative activity in natural processes and its escaping scientific detection. Many have thus concluded that recourse to God is inadmissible, unscientific and unintelligible. What can I say? I now think otherwise. I have emphasized ignorance in our knowledge: A thousand Frenchmen may be wrong in their surmising!

Unexpected occurrences: **God's signature?**

BlueInk Review of *Existential Ruminations*

Gentry Thomason's *Existential Ruminations* is a collection of "poemographs," which he explains are "attempts to articulate my *thoughts* in some *rhythmical* manner that approximate [sic] recognizable ordinary speech." He shares that he does not "typically employ poetic artifice in these poemographs" and that they are 14 lines long, a container which he "absorbed from the English sonnet form" as an apt amount of space for the expression of most ideas.

The collection is separated into five main sections titled "Existence and Eternity," "Truth and Reality," "God, Religion, and the Supernatural," "Self and Others," "Character, Love and Vision," plus a "Postscript" and then some lists and miscellany.

The poemographs are often contemplative, as in "Feelings (and Words)," which begins: "Which comes first: feelings or words?" and moralistic, as in "Forever (question)," which begins: "What is God doing/ with the daily thousands/ who enter into death/ with questionable, erroneous behaviors/ that are ostensibly unsound/ and lacking wholesome morality?"

One of the most interesting poemographs relates three "traumatic afflictions" that resulted in hospitalizations. During the last hospitalization, the narrator "heard a Voice/ that frightened [him] into a serious mending/ of [his] waywardness and obdurate unbelief." Then the narrator goes to Confession and is "struck with spiritual lightning" and experiences physical transportation "traversing four miles in under three seconds," and knows that "Only God could engineer such Astonishment." That piece then colors the rest of the collection and its questing tone with a spiritual gravitas.

As indicated by the title, this is a book about existence and God's role in it, if any. The speaker examines his doubts throughout. As Thomason acknowledges, the work is not artistic. It's filled with abstract, prose-like language and is often didactic, rather than allowing readers to draw their own conclusions.

Still, it might appeal to those who want to journey along with an unsentimental yet religious pilgrim who isn't afraid of harboring an expansive sense of skepticism in his search for the truth.

This is my reply to the unidentified "blueink review" of Existential Ruminations (hereafter ER).

1. This reviewer's "[sic]" in the second line is incorrect: "attempts ... approximate" is correct, not "attempts ...approximates" [sic]. This lapse shows this reviewers <u>precious</u> arrogance and <u>pose</u> of superiority.

2. That I acknowledge I do <u>not</u> "typically employ poetic artifice" in my poemographs does not confess that "the work is not artistic"! I contend there is much "art" in my poemographs, much "art" in the expression of "thought". Original thought! This reviewer shows a lack of imagination, appreciation and recognition of my artistry, that my writing is a hybrid of free verse and non-fiction, that it is original and structurally non-traditional.

3. "The poemographs are often contemplative" is inaccurate: My verse is uniformly contemplative. See my book's title: Existential Ruminations.

4. I do acknowledge that poemographs are sometimes "moralistic". However, the one selection cited, "Forever (question)", suggests to me this reviewer's <u>unease</u> at that poemograph's idea expression. Other selections might have been better chosen.

5. Paragraph four of this review fails to note apodictically the confessional tone of my entire book. The reviewer does acknowledge ER's "spiritual gravitas". Much more could have been made of that observation, showing insight.

6. "It's filled with abstract, prose-like language [yes] and is often didactic [?], rather than allowing readers to draw their own conclusions." This statement is pejorative {faultfinding, disparaging}. Readers are uniformly <u>invited</u> to draw their own conclusions: Note poemographs like "Examine (the Evidence)" for such encouragement. Note also the 269 question marks inviting reflection.

7. This reviewer might have <u>recognized</u> in his/her proficiency some similarity in my writing (albeit the centering of content lines) to the verse of Walt Whitman.

8. "Still, it might appeal to those who" clearly expresses this reviewer's bias toward my kind of original expressioning.

9. This review is lacking in a profound sense of sympathy, is intent on expressing overarching superiority, and is remarkably intellectually uncomplimentary.

10. In my <u>Rouges' Gallery</u> the Greek myth of Procrustes--he who required way-farers to fit into a bed of his determination—articulates a <u>reductive</u> and lethal mold. Unhappily, this is the pit into which this reviewer has fallen.

11. Finally, this reviewer has failed to wrestle with and fully disclose the profound essence of ER: a) the significance of my miracle experience and its <u>extraordinary</u> implications; b) the drama of doubt versus hope, of eternal life and death; c) mankind's profound and vast ignorance of its existence on this planet; d) the mystery surrounding the evocation of God; e) the nature of evil and our continued inability to resolve its occurrence; f) the mystery of mankind's epistemic distance from God; g) the parallelism of my miracle experience, my automobile crash survival, and my much earlier high school football catching experience; these, among many others.

What is Dying?

I am standing on the sea shore. A ship sails and spreads
her white sails to the morning breeze and starts for the Ocean.
She is an object of beauty and I stand watching her
till at last she fades on the horizon,
and someone at my side says, "She is gone." Gone where?
Gone from my sight, that is all; she is just as large in the masts,
hull and spars as she was when I saw her,
and just as able to bear her load of living freight to its destination.

The diminished size and total loss of sight is in me, not in her;
and just at the moment when someone at my side says,
"She is gone," there are others who are watching her coming,
and other voices take up a glad shout,
"There she comes," and that is dying.

Words of wisdom
By: Daniel P. Cronin

Compassionate
(Caring)

Mankind needs to be more loving.
World leaders need to be more caring.
Self-aggrandizement is not the answer.
More cooperation is what is called for,
less dependence on "our loving God".
Perhaps "our God" has thus grown restless,
wants all mankind to assume the mantle
of the attributions we have given Him:
The time has come, He may be saying
"You must grow up, act out those blessings"
we ask of Him––must assume His mantle
of being wise and being mature,
give up self-seeking
and learn to exemplify what we ask of Him:
Loving others with compassionate caring.

Life
(and Eternity)

My focus in this book
has been on Life and Eternity
--the complexities of this life
and our encompassing ignorance
about what may follow at death:
We can immerse ourselves
in comforting beliefs
that are found in scriptures
holding fast to promises
to assuage uncertainties
--but we really don't know
if glory awaits us
when we depart this world:
Hope springs eternal:
--it is nice to think so?

Gentry Thomason: Brief Autobiography

I was born and raised in Liberty, Missouri. My greatest love growing up was playing football. My family moved to San Diego, California in 1956, but I returned to Liberty to play football and graduate from Liberty High. During my succeeding college years and thereafter I have been absorbed with reading and thinking about the subjects of philosophy, psychology and religion, among many others.

After graduating from college and before entering the U.S. Army in early 1964 I spent the summer working at selling Great Books of the Western World cold canvass door to door and was honored as the most prolific junior salesman. I was then drafted into the Army and completed Basic Training at Fort Ord, California. From there I went to Fort Benning, Georgia where I completed Officer Candidate School (OCS) and Airborne Training (parachuting/jump school). After completing active duty at Fort Ord I was employed by Washington Inventory Service as a Management Trainee, then served as a Branch Manager in their Hayward, California office. I worked for WIS for approximately two years, then attended graduate school at San Diego State University where I completed a Master's Degree in English Literature.

My academic background has included graduation from William Jewell College (B.A. in Liberal Arts--Economics and Philosophy); Army Officer Candidate School and Airborne Training; San Diego State University (M.A. in English Literature); and Northern Illinois University (Graduate Assistant in English Literature--where I taught Freshman Literature and Composition).

After leaving graduate school at NIU I sought employment at Community Colleges in California and discovered they were hiring persons with Ph. D. Degrees or otherwise those with more extensive teaching experience. Subsequently, I worked as an Administrative Assistant with The City of San Diego in their Engineering Department. I worked with the City for several years, then moved on to other employments before starting my own window cleaning business in 1984. That employment supported my living for four and one-half years before I commenced teaching, at the secondary school level, for the Los Angeles Unified School District from 1988 to 2011. I taught all six grade levels, 7 through 12, including Honors courses and Advanced Literature and Advanced Composition at Thomas Jefferson High School.

My published works include my Master's Thesis The Metamorphosis of Nick Adams (an analysis of Ernest Hemingway's first major literary character); Rogues' Gallery (a study of the relevance of Greek Mythology to contemporary life and living); and Existential Ruminations (reflections on existence and eternity, truth and reality, God, religion and the supernatural, self and others, and character, love and vision).

At my retirement from teaching in Los Angeles I returned to my original hometown of Liberty, Missouri where I have resided since. For the past several years I have composed the poemographs of Existential Ruminations (ER) published in 2022 (and slightly revised in 2023). That work incorporates reflections on experiences I endured during the 1970s-most especially a reversal of traveling in August of 1979 which I acknowledge was a literal miracle. The balance of ER encompasses reflections on my readings in philosophy, psychology and religion (among other subjects) over the past six plus decades. The preponderance of that thinking focused on the subjects of God, love, death, the reliability of scriptures, and a possible future life in Eternity. My decades of reading in the "forest of doubt" and my miracle experience have moved me from being a hardcore atheist to a puzzled believer in God's reality and the possibility of life after death.

Index

246

If you would like to contact the author,
please reply to the following website:
gentrysruminations.com